70115330

THE MAKING OF A MINDFUL MARRIAGE

Mindfulness for Christian Couples

Ted W. Raddell, Ph.D.

authorHOUSE®

AuthorHouse™
1663 Liberty Drive
Bloomington, IN 47403
www.authorhouse.com
Phone: 833-262-8899

Published by AuthorHouse 04/19/2021

ISBN: 978-1-6655-2315-8 (sc)
ISBN: 978-1-6655-2314-1 (e)

Library of Congress Control Number: 2021908071

To my wife, Kathleen, for her steadfast love, support, prayers and friendship over the years. Thank you for all your efforts to create a more mindful marriage together.

Contents

Preface xi

Chapter 1   Consider the Sparrows … 1
Chapter 2   The Breath 13
Chapter 3   Understanding and Appreciating
              Differences... 20
Chapter 4   Transforming Swords into Plowshares....... 32
Chapter 5   Betrayal and Trust 43
Chapter 6   Parenting 50
Chapter 7   Sexual Intimacy... 62
Chapter 8   Communicating Mindfully 70
Chapter 9   Spirituality and Marriage...........................81
Chapter 10   The Great Commission............................. 89

PREFACE

According to the founders of Retrovai, a Christian marriage program, marriages typically go through four phases: romance, disillusionment, misery, and reawakening. Many never make it through the second or third stage. No one on their wedding day imagines they could be part of the staggering divorce statistics. We are filled with hope, excitement, and expectations. Some expectations are conscious, such as "It's going to be so wonderful to live together." Other expectations are subconscious, such as "My spouse is going to fulfill all of my emotional needs perfectly." As time passes, we discover strengths and weaknesses, insecurities, sinfulness, and blind spots, which prompt disillusionment. They may begin to think, *This is not what I signed up for when I decided to marry!*

To successfully process through the phases and achieve reawakening requires willingness and effort. Should you decide to embark on this adventure, you will discover and master one of our best inner resources for marital success and satisfaction. In reading *The Making of a Mindful Marriage*, you will come to understand what mindfulness is, practice it in a variety of ways, and learn how to apply it to your marital relationship. However, just as reading a book on exercise doesn't make you physically fit, if the words of this book remain on the page and are not incorporated into your day-to-day activities and interactions, they are unlikely to transform your marriage into all that it can be.

I have heard it said that success in marriage is not so much about *finding* the right person as it is about *being* the right person. Awakening to this best possible version of yourself is a natural by-product of mindfulness meditation. This, in turn, assists us in fulfilling God's calling for our lives. We discover the secret to being *fully present* to our spouses and the courage to love them the way they deserve as unique, irreplaceable creations of God.

Mindfulness is not inherently religious. It is merely a pathway to human effectiveness. However, it has the potential to enhance our spirituality and prayer life as well as the quality of our marital relationship. Non-Christians also find the practice of mindfulness strengthens their marital relationships because it is a scientifically validated exercise for your brain. However, I chose to write this book from a Christian perspective partly to incorporate key related scriptures but mostly because being mindful to keep Christ at the center of your marriage fosters grace and perseverance. Regardless of one's faith background, readers will benefit from the principles and exercises contained in this book.

So how is one to use this book? I suggest reading one chapter per week. This allows you time to practice the concepts and exercises for three to five days before moving on to the next chapter. Taking this approach allows opportunities to put the ideas into practice and develop some sense of mastery before progressing to more advanced applications, such as when you feel angry or betrayed. I pray that your marriage will be richly blessed as a result of accepting this challenge to create a mindful marriage!

Chapter 1

Consider the Sparrows ...

With our busy lifestyles, moments of quiet reflection are rare. If you are raising children, it may seem like weeks go by without an opportunity for uninterrupted silence. Quiet is healthy for us spiritually, emotionally, cognitively, and even physically. However, the goal of mindfulness is not to escape life but to embrace it.

Mindfulness refers to attending purposefully to what you are doing without evaluating the experience as positive or negative. It often involves focusing on one thing and remaining in the moment throughout. Instead, we are often encouraged to multitask at both work and home. Multitasking is the ability to do multiple activities simultaneously, such as talking on the phone while working on the computer. Multitasking has benefits in certain settings—I was always amazed how my wife, Kathleen, could wash the dishes, feed the baby, and correct one of our children's homework, all at the same time!

The problem with me is that I can become an automaton, going through the motions of one activity while my mind is on something else. An embarrassing example of this would be conversing with my wife while watching a sporting event on TV. Besides being rude, I'm really not attending well to either experience. Mindfulness encourages something different. If I am eating, I should just eat; if I am mowing the lawn, I should really mow it; and if I'm talking with my wife, I should devote my full attention to her.

Couples in Crisis

Married life presents many challenges. In doing marital therapy and in observing married friends and family members, I often sense great discouragement, reflected in statements such as "I'm trying to do what she wants," "I wish he and I could just get along," "It's as if we lead separate lives," "The more I try to fix the problem, the worse it gets," and "Sometimes I just feel like giving up … like, is it really worth it?" I believe it is worth it, but then I'm one of those who no longer feel discouraged.

The problem that needs fixing may not lie in my spouse but in how I react to interpersonal difficulties. Many spouses have left one relationship only to carry the same problems into the next one. Developing the ability to understand and accept our differences, and even our own distractions and reactions, can go a long way toward cultivating the inner resources needed to grow a strong marriage.

As a society, we have bought a bill of goods that suggests "life should be easy," "if it feels good, do it," and "no one should ever suffer unnecessarily." Advertisements continually bombard us with messages such as "you deserve a break today." With more than half of all marriages ending in divorce, most of us have personally known several divorced people. The familiarity of divorce leads many people to believe that if you are unhappy in your marriage, you should get out—Mr. and Mrs. So-and-So did!

Paul Simon observed this phenomenon in his lyrics for the song "Train in the Distance." Simon tells an all-too-common story of a man and a woman who pursue each other, fall in love, marry, experience a variety of disagreements, and become disenchanted with their marriage:

Two disappointed believers.

Two people playing the game.

Negotiations and love songs

Are often mistaken for one and the same.

In the end, the couple assumes the grass is greener on the other side of the fence—or as the song puts it:

The thought that life could be better

Is woven indelibly

Into our hearts and our brains.

Though many married individuals fall into the trap of believing they would be happier with someone else, the sociological data does not support this notion. Most of us know that the divorce rate in the United States is 51 percent. However, that is for first marriages. Statistics show that the divorce rate is 67 percent for second marriages and 74 percent for third marriages. Therefore, the idea that an individual will be happier if he or she finds someone new is unlikely. If people don't deal with their issues with intimacy in their existing relationship, they may very likely carry the same tendencies into the next and repeat history.

Over the past few decades, the traditional family has been increasingly denigrated, creating widespread apathy and resignation that diminish basic Judeo-Christian values. People fail to realize that pain is inevitable, but misery is optional. In other words, disappointments, hurt feelings, loss, anger, and physical pain are simply a function of being human. Misery is what *I* add to the experience as a result of *my* expectations, misperceptions, assumptions, and rigid or negative thoughts and beliefs. Believe me, no one can make me miserable the way I can!

At this point,you may be wondering where to begin to change your response to a significant relationship. We start with the bare bones of human awareness.

The Raisin

Go to the cupboard right now, get a single raisin, and bring it back to where you are sitting. If you don't have a raisin, an M&M, a tangerine section, or a peanut will suffice. Quietly hold the raisin in your hand. Study this object as if you had never seen one before: observe the color, notice the weight, sense the texture of it. Gently close your eyes, and place the raisin in your mouth, but don't chew it right away.

Isn't it interesting how you intuitively know how to move it around in your mouth as you explore the texture? Notice how light it is. Become aware of the size, shape, and malleability of this bit of food in your mouth. Thoughtfully begin to chew the raisin, eating it almost as slowly as you can and simply noticing what that is like.

What did you notice? Was there something about the texture of the raisin that struck your interest? Did you notice how much saliva you produced? Did the size and shape change in quality? When did you first become aware of the flavor? When I do this simple exercise, I'm often struck by how much flavor can exist within a single raisin.

This is how I typically introduce the idea of mindfulness. I have to admit, it is a strange suggestion to recommend spending several minutes eating a single raisin! Most of us eat a handful at a time. It is also unusual to just eat. What other activities do you typically do while eating? Talking, reading the newspaper, straightening the house, driving, planning your day, watching TV ... the list is endless. Once I was so absorbed in what I was reading during lunch that when I looked down at my plate, I was surprised to find it empty. *What happened to my meal?* I wondered. I actually did ingest it, but I never tasted one morsel!

A more common example of mindlessness occurs when you drive the same route to work every day. About twenty years ago, I was working at a rehabilitation facility that was a half hour away from home by freeway. Several times a year, I would arrive at my office and have no idea how I got there. I would not remember one sign, car, or song on the radio during my entire drive to work that morning. When I stopped to wonder where I had been during that time, I realized I was processing something that happened earlier or anticipating what I was going to do once I got to work. I guess I was on autopilot while driving, but as with my empty plate, I missed the actual experience.

With mindfulness practice, we not only learn how to remain in the moment, we come to realize that each moment is valid, a gift worthy of one's attention. Some wonder what they should use as a focal point to learn mindfulness. A simple scripture verse such as "Be still and know that I am God" (Psalms 46:10 New International

Version [NIV]) synchronized with the breath can be very powerful. However, a picture, word, sound, or even a single leaf could represent an opportunity to practice. Regardless of what I choose as a focal point, I find that within several seconds, my mind still wanders, or I may be distracted by a sound, thought, sensation, judgment, memory, or some other experience. It is very helpful to know what to do with distractions, as they are so common.

I often use a metaphor to describe the handling of distractions. Imagine going to the woods and discovering a rock in the midst of a stream. You decide to pause and employ the rock as a focal point. So there you are noticing the size, shape, and color or how water flows over or around the rock, when a leaf falls off a tree, lands in the stream, and floats past the rock. When the leaf comes into your field of vision, you have a decision to make. One option is to follow the distraction, the leaf. You might think, *Check out that leaf. It's floating on top of the water like a little canoe. I wonder how far it will go. I bet this stream connects with the river … and the river into the lake … That reminds me of the time I went boating with my brother …* This is a perfectly normal human experience.

What you may not realize is that you have other options when the leaf comes into your awareness. You may be tempted to try to block out the distraction. However, meditation never involves blocking things out. To the contrary, acknowledge it. You might say to yourself, "It's okay; it's just a leaf." You don't even have to name it. You could say, "It's just a thing" or "It's just a thought," even if the leaf were to get stuck in some sticks right next to the rock. Imagine a bright-red autumn leaf floating tantalizingly close to the rock just crying out for your attention. You could apply the same accepting attitude. In fact, you could treat this thought, emotion, or sensation as if it were an unexpected guest. Even if it is a preoccupation that ordinarily you would ruminate about on and off throughout the day, try thinking, *Welcome! Pull up a chair and stick around as long as you wish, but for the time being, I'm staying with the rock.*

In addition to distractions, a second, equally widespread challenge exists for those unfamiliar with mindfulness. We spend countless hours upset about things that have happened in the past or worried about the future. However, if I'm in the past or I'm in the future then what am I liable to miss out on? That's right! The present—which is all I really have if you think about it. I cannot change the past! I cannot predict what will happen tomorrow, let alone in the distant future! All I really have is this moment, right now, writing on this piece of paper.

This is not to suggest that we'll live *for* the moment or simply "eat and drink for tomorrow we die" (1 Corinthians 15:32 NIV). Rather, we are to live *in* the moment or, as we are instructed in Ephesians 4, to "live a life worthy of the calling you have received" (Ephesians 4:1 NIV). Therefore, if you are currently employed as a garbage collector, then be the best garbage collector you can be. This is your calling for today. This does not mean you must always remain in that job. However, if you've given your life to God, and this is where He has you, embrace it! This philosophy was modeled for us by St. Therese of Liseaux, who demonstrated that we can serve God by doing our best in the mundane activities of life. This is often now referred to as "the little way." She has been quoted as saying, "I may not be able to do great things, but I can do little things with great love."

Of Birds and Flowers

Have you ever been anxious or worried? I know I have. It seems anxiety is ubiquitous, as everyone is familiar with this experience. Fortunately, Jesus addressed this very issue with His friends in His Sermon on the Mount.

> So my counsel is: Don't worry about things—food, drink, and clothes. For you already have life and a body—and they are far more important than what to eat and wear. Look at the birds! They don't worry about what to eat—they don't need to sow or reap or store up food—for your heavenly Father feeds them. And you are far more valuable to him than they are. Will all your worries add a single moment to your life?
>
> And why worry about your clothes? Look at the field lilies! They don't worry about theirs. Yet King Solomon in all his glory was not clothed as beautifully as they. And if God cares so wonderfully for flowers that are here today and gone tomorrow, won't he more surely care for you, O men of little faith? (Matthew 6:25–30, The Children's Living Bible)

Herein Jesus

1) captures the essence of mindfulness for His followers
2) Illustrates One Of Its Greatest Benefits—Freedom From Anxiety
3) Teaches Us An Effective Exercise We Can Employ To Develop This Inner Resource

Jesus captures the essence of mindfulness by encouraging us to focus our full attention on one thing—in most translations, it is a sparrow—while remaining in the moment and reserving judgment. It is almost humorous to ponder the question, "How much has this bird worried about his career, marriage, finances, health, and so on?" Not one iota! Why? Because the sparrow intuitively knows God, his creator, will care for him. Yet you are far more precious to God than some bird!

Of all the benefits of developing a mindfulness practice, the first one we typically experience is greater peacefulness. Mindfulness has been a pathway to enhanced physical health, parenting, weight management, and grief recovery and is even an empirically validated method for preventing relapse of depression. Yet reduction in anxiety is one of the most palpable and commonly cited benefits initially. So how does one practically accomplish this? Read on ...

In the passage from Matthew's gospel, Jesus identifies one method with which we can begin to master the skill of mindfulness. By focusing on one of God the Father's creations in nature, we are gently guided back to the basics. We are instructed in some simple yet essential truths. Things of nature do not suffer from anxiety. They exist in the moment. They focus on the task at hand. For all else, they are "FROG," which stands for "fully reliant on God." In the remainder of Matthew 6, Christ distills the passage into one simple idea that could become a foundation for a stronger, healthier, more satisfying marriage.

> So don't be anxious for tomorrow. God will take
> care of your tomorrow too. Live one day at a time.
> —Matthew 6:34 (CLB)

Mindfulness Exercise #1

Mindful Listening

Now that you know what the basics of mindfulness entail, let's begin to experiment with a simple practice exercise. Ihope you have tried the raisin exercise already. If not, grab a single raisin from the cupboard and give it a try. Another simple foray into mindfulness is mindful listening. Stop at a nearby park for a walk, or, if easier, step out into your yard. Pause in the busyness of your day at a place where you can have a few moments alone. Gently allow your eyes to close and simply notice the various sounds of the day. You might hear traffic in the distance or a neighbor's lawn mower running. Either way, do not judge the sound as good or bad. Rather, listen with curiosity as if you have never heard that sound before. As you continue to stand and listen, you may hear a bird. Sometimes we can hear the breeze moving through the trees. You may get distracted and begin thinking about something you need to do later today. Observe that thought as just a thought and know you can come back to it later. Gently guide your awareness back to the sounds of the day and greet them with a sense of compassion without any need to explain or even identify what the sound may be. Notice how the sound may increase or fade over time. Finally, take a full breath and cleanse it out. Congratulate yourself for devoting a few minutes to meditation this very first week of your adventure. You may even find yourself spontaneously thanking God for your ability to hear, which is very easy to take for granted.

> He said to them, "Come away by yourselves
> to a deserted place and rest awhile."
> —Mark 6:31 (New American Bible Revised)

CHAPTER 2

The Breath

Remaining in the Moment

Have you ever watched professional golf on television and wondered in amazement how the top pros could strike the ball so consistently well? Many hours on the practice range certainly help, but all the pros dedicate many hours to practicing their swing. What makes the difference between competitor and champion is mindfulness—the ability of the athlete to focus on one thing, stay in the moment, and reserve judgment. If I am preparing to tee off and am dwelling on how poorly I putted on the last hole, I'm not in the moment, and my negative judgment shifts my mental set. Likewise, if I am worried about getting the ball over the lake, I am getting ahead of myself, and my anxiety will cause my muscles to tighten, which changes my swing. However, if I can stay in the present with the simple mechanics of this particular stroke, I will perform as well as my skills will allow. Chances are good the ball will land in the fairway.

A strong corollary exists between the pro golfer in the

middle of the final round of a major tournament and a husband trying to gracefully handle a difficult issue with his wife. The husband may have the communication or relationship skills but struggle to apply them when really needed in the marriage. Consider the dilemma of Tom, a twenty-six-year-old computer technician, who is upset that his wife of two years, Cami, likes to go to a local tavern every Thursday night with her female friends to sing karaoke while Tom stays home and watches their two-year-old daughter. Tom experiences intense worry, anger, and distrust regarding his wife's outings. He typically stews for days, as he doesn't want to come across as jealous or controlling. He decides to keep his feelings to himself but ends up giving Cami the cold shoulder for the entire weekend. Cami gets angry and questions why she stays in the relationship if Tom cannot trust her to go out with friends.

During individual counseling, Tom is able to express his feelings pretty well but becomes distraught when the issue with his wife comes up in the kitchen at home. Like the golfer, if Tom can focus on one thing (how he feels when his wife goes out on Thursdays), stay in the moment (not bring up past issues or assume she will go out every Thursday for the next twenty years), and reserve judgment (not evaluate or criticize but consider her feelings as valid), he is considerably more equipped to discuss his concerns calmly, understand his wife's perspective, and explore options together.

One cannot walk onto the golf course during a major tournament and expect to be mindful unless one has developed that inner resource through practice in the weeks and months prior to the event. Most people value the idea of living life one day at a time or handling challenges one moment at a time. Yet few actually achieve this approach to life. Christian mindfulness is the pathway that enables us to put this philosophy into practice in our daily life. In fact, everything I do today could be a meditation!

A good place to begin is by practicing a simple breathing meditation. As with the raisin, this is something best experienced rather than just read about or considered intellectually. If you wanted to become more proficient at shooting foul shots in basketball, you are much more likely to develop a smooth, consistent stroke from practicing this shot rather than just reading about it. My suggestion is to first read this section and then put it aside. Thus you can fully immerse yourself in the experience versus remaining in a thinking state of mind.

The Gift of the Breath

Find a comfortable position with good posture, and gently allow your eyes to close … Simply begin by becoming aware of what it is like to be in this room. Notice the sound of the air circulating through the windows or vents, activity in nearby rooms, or even the sounds outside, such as a bus, a siren, or a car door closing … Experience the temperature of this place. Notice the warmth or coolness of the room and how that feels against your hands or face … Become aware of what it's like to be sitting in this chair. Sense the feeling of the back of the chair against your back or how the seat cushion supports your legs. Notice where your feet touch the soles of your shoes, which connect with the floor. Even experience where your body may connect with itself—if your arms are folded or legs are crossed, what are the sensations at these places of contact?

In a similar fashion, become aware of the breath and where the breath rests in your body. It may be up high in the chest, in the midsection around your stomach, or down low, in the belly. Wherever it is at this moment is perfectly fine … Notice how the air moves in and out of your body as you breathe in through the nose and out through the mouth or whatever way is most comfortable for you … Isn't it interesting how you can move the breath from one area to another? First breathe into the chest area. Then move that same breath into the midsection and perhaps all the way into the belly before releasing all the old air out into the room. Invite yourself to experience the quality of each breath. Some breaths are longer, while some breaths are shorter; some may be smooth, and some may be choppy; yet each breath is equally valid. Each breath is equally worthy of one's attention … Notice how the stomach gently rises with the in breath and falls with the out breath. Do not worry about doing it right, but just give yourself permission to experience the fullness and richness of each breath.

Become aware of each part of the breath … the inhale … the turn … the exhale … the pause … the inhale, and so on. Pay careful attention to the pause. What are the sensations that you are experiencing in your body as you pause between one breath and the next?

Now, with the next breath, you will, naturally, inhale, but as you exhale, think, *One*. Before long, you will take another breath in, but as you breathe out, count this as *Two*, and the next exhale as *Three*. Go all the way up to *Four*, and then cycle back to "one" and "two" and so on so that you are simply counting each out breath in sets of four … If at any point you should lose count, pay this no mind. Feel free to begin again with "one" whenever you wish. (Long pause.)

At times, a thought may enter your mind, and that is not unusual. Simply acknowledge that thought as "just a thought" and then gently return your awareness back to the breath … back to the smooth, rhythmical pattern of your breathing and the simple counting of each individual exhale, knowing that you can start again with "one" whenever you want to. (Long pause.)

From time to time, a sound or a sensation may capture your attention, and that is very common. Simply focus on that sound or feeling … until it recedes … and then gently escort your awareness back to the breath … back to the smooth, almost wavelike, pattern of your breathing. Resume the simple counting of each out breath. (Long pause.)

Every once in a while, you may come upon a thought you find enticing and wish to contemplate. That can happen to anybody. But, again, choose to acknowledge that thought as "just a thought," and like the leaf on the stream, allow it to float on by, knowing you can return to it later as you gently ease your mind back to this moment, back to the breath. Embrace the fullness and richness of each breath … and return to the simple counting of each exhale, knowing that you can start again with whatever number you wish. (Long pause.)

When you are ready … you will slowly and gradually begin to feel more alert and awake. As you begin to feel more alert, your eyes will naturally want to open, and you'll be ready for whatever you want to do next.

After this fifteen- to twenty-minute period of practice,

it can be helpful to simply reflect on what that experience was like for you. Sometimes it is very difficult, while other times, it can be deeply relaxing. Occasionally, I'll have so many thoughts racing through my mind, it seems almost impossible to focus on one thing. Regardless of how it goes, acknowledge it for what it is without labeling it as good or bad. Herein lies a wonderful opportunity to practice nonjudgment. This is not to say we forever abandon judgments. However, engaging in judgmental attitudes and expectations in our marriage is very different than invoking God's wisdom in our interactions as we will learn later in the book. Practicing a simple breathing meditation daily can serve as a stepping-stone to experiencing, understanding, and fostering greater mindfulness which will lay the foundation on which to build stronger relationships and enjoy greater closeness with our spouse and with God.

Sometimes when I am practicing this mindful breathing exercise, I find myself just thanking God for each individual breath. It is intriguing to me that I can go for days without once thinking about my breath, but if I did not breathe for three to four minutes, I wouldn't even be alive. I was recently reading a book that was describing the spiritual exercises of St. Ignatius of Loyola. One of the predominant themes of this disciple is to learn to see or experience the sacred in the simple, such as studying a drop of water on a flower petal, observing a young child playing in the sand, or watching a spider spin a web. In devoting hours of practice to this spiritual exercise, we come to celebrate God's creativity and playfulness. How powerful it would be if I could view my wife of thirty years with that same wonder and appreciation.

Mindfulness Exercise #2

The Breath Meditation

Now that you have been instructed in the breath exercise, I want to encourage you to practice it once a day for a week. Although any time of day can be a good time to practice the breath meditation, I recommend trying it in the first hour of your day, as it sets the tone for your day and as troubling issues arise, we are better equipped to respond mindfully. If it is easier to be guided through the exercise, I suggest recording the instructions from this chapter on your phone by speaking slowly and with pauses between each statement to allow the words or ideas to resonate. This way, each morning, you can just hit play and follow along. Some people will make a recording for their spouse or find a suitable mindful breathing app or exercise on the internet.

O present moment, you belong to me, whole and entire. I desire to use you as best I can. And although I am weak and small, you grant me the grace of your omnipotence. And so, trusting in your mercy, I walk through life like a little child, offering you each day this heart burning for love for your greater glory.
—St. Faustina Kowalska, Diary, *Divine Mercy in My Soul, Notebook*

CHAPTER 3

Understanding and Appreciating Differences

Viva La Difference

Early in my career, when I would interview a new couple coming for therapy, I'd get excited about the potential within them to renew their marriage through the application of mindfulness to their everyday life. Occasionally, one might respond, "Our marriage is falling apart, and *you want to teach us about meditation?*" I realize it seems like a stretch to grasp the connection at first, but the process of rewriting love stories with troubled couples is often a leap of faith in itself. In recent years, I rarely begin marital therapy with mindfulness training, but I always get to it because, over time, it seems to be one of the most powerful resources in understanding and appreciating each other as unique creations of God.

Now that you have begun a daily practice of mindfulness meditation, we can begin to explore ways to apply this to enhancing your relationship with your spouse. Approximately fifteen years ago, my wife, Kathleen, and I were discussing some issues in our relationship, and she said, "I'd appreciate it if you would hold me more."

I replied, "That's fine. I like to do that. Maybe being married all these years and having kids, we've just gotten out of the habit or taken the relationship for granted."

It wasn't really a fight. It was more of a serious conversation. About three weeks later, Kathleen was cleaning our bedroom and came across one of my little reminder lists on a scrap of paper on my dresser. It was not unusual to find one of these lists in a pocket or next to my bathroom sink, as I am notoriously absent-minded. Kathleen read the list to see if it was something to keep or pitch and discovered the following items:

1) Buy paint for hallway
2) Mow lawn
3) Hold Kathy more
4) Get batteries for clock

Well, let me tell you, she was miffed. She came to me holding out the list and demanded, "What is this?"

I clearly got the feeling I was in trouble, but I wasn't sure why. I responded, "That is one of my lists of things I want to remember to do."

She said, "No, this third point to 'hold Kathy more'?"

I defended myself, "Don't you remember? We just had this conversation a few weeks ago!"

Every woman I have ever told this story knows exactly what my wife said next and completely agrees with her statement. My wife asserted, "Ted, you shouldn't have to write this down (hold Kathy more) like it's some kind of chore you have to do! You should just want to do it!"

Normally, I'd get defensive at this point and exclaim, "Hey, I was trying to do something nice, and you don't give a crap!" But all of a sudden, a light bulb went off in my head. I had a mindful moment and realized this was a perfect example of hemispheric differences between men and women. Neurological studies have indicated that most men rely heavier on the left side of the brain (specialized for logic, reasoning, strategy, sequentially ordered events, and so on), whereas the majority of women rely more on the right side of the brain (specialized for creativity, emotional processing, relationships, spatial abilities, and so on). This idea that affection should just naturally flow from within is clearly a right-brained phenomenon, whereas writing "hold Kathy more" on a reminder list is clearly a left-brained phenomenon.

My wife was upset with me, but for a change, I didn't get defensive that day. I just listened. I understood why she was reacting as she was, even though it was totally different from my perspective. I was acting strategically while she was processing information through an emotional filter in her brain. In fact, I left "hold Kathy more" on my to-do list for a few more weeks because it was a helpful reminder of something important—that is, to practice being in the moment in my marriage. The other blessing was that physical expressions of affection were becoming "second nature" again. When we would be shopping, I'd hold her hand; when driving, I'd place my hand on her knee; and if she would be standing in the kitchen, I'd come up behind her and gently embrace her.

I also realized I needed to find a way to access my own emotional filter. If I was going to learn to understand my wife's reactions and communicate in a language in which she was fluent, I needed to become more adept at drawing from the right hemisphere of the brain. Having more fibers in the corpus callosum, which connects the two sides of the brain, women may have an advantage in the ease of access to the typically male-dominated left hemisphere functions. However, anyone who has ever injured their dominant hand can attest that you can learn to use your nondominant one. Similarly, even though it will always be my natural inclination to draw from the left side of the brain and respond to my wife with logic and rationality, I can learn over time to draw from the emotional-creative right side and respond with greater sensitivity and relational affirmation. As my older sister once wisely suggested, "Sometimes it is more important to be loving than right."

> I may be able to speak the languages of men and even of angels, but if I have not love, my speech is not more than a noisy gong or a clanging bell. I may have the gift of inspired preaching; I may have all knowledge and understand all secrets; I may have all the faith needed to move mountains—but if I have not love, I am nothing. I may give away everything I have, and even give up my body to be burned—but if I have not love, it does me no good. (1 Corinthians 13:1–3, *Good News for Modern Man*, 3rd ed.)

What fascinates me most about the whole "hold Kathy more" incident is not that we disagreed about the issue. The truth is we both agreed that demonstrating more affection was important to the health of our marriage. However, our ways of getting there were *totally* different. I approached the matter strategically. I viewed it as a task or challenge and, therefore, utilized logic and intellect in changing my behavior. Like any good cognitive behavioral psychologist, I thought, *Come up with a plan, Ted, to cue yourself to remember.* Kathleen, in contrast, seemed to be suggesting that if one attends to one's feelings, more frequent expressions of love and affection would be a natural outcome. The only problem with this perspective is that I rarely pay close attention to my emotions, whereas this comes very natural to her. She is much more mindful of her emotional state in the moment. As you will discover later in the book, mindfulness can aid us in becoming more observant of our own emotions and enable us to strike that balance between thinking mind and emotional mind, referred to by psychologist Marcia Linehan as "wise mind."

So Long Self

Understanding and appreciating your differences also means understanding yourself better through self-observation and recognizing your human preoccupation with self-gratification. Have you ever desired some time away from your spouse? Have you ever wished your spouse would change to better meet your needs? These expectations are often a reflection of an imbalance inside oneself we call codependency. Codependency is when my feelings hinge entirely on how someone else is feeling. If that person is happy and treating me well, then I am satisfied and feel momentarily worthwhile. If the other is sad, angry, or unsettled, I am filled with anxiety and insecurity. If I am always reaching out to another to know I am okay, I am leaning forward and liable to tip over. However, if I push away out of fear of abandonment or rejection, I am leaning backward and the slightest disappointment will topple me over, or I will exist in a state of isolation. However, if Christ is at my center, I am more balanced and can tolerate emotional changes in my spouse better. I carry this moving center within me, and I can move in any direction without fear of falling. I can respond meaningfully to my spouse's emotional state out of love and understanding.

So often, there is a pushing or pulling occurring in relationship to one's spouse. I am either pushing away to achieve more space for what I want to do, pushing my agenda, or pushing for more freedom, or I am pulling at my partner—that is, being needy, enmeshed, clingy, or demanding. If I am constantly withdrawing or frequently needy, I am out of balance. Daily practice of mindfulness meditation can also help restore that balance, as it teaches us how to notice and acknowledge these tendencies without giving in to the impulse. I become more aware and accepting of these temporary states. Through mindfulness practice, we can also learn selflessness. The song "So Long Self" by the contemporary Christian music group Mercy Me describes this decision to abandon self so as to fully devote one's life to Christ. The lyricist has a dialogue with his own ego and decides "There's just no room for two. So you are gonna have to move. So long, self." St. Ignatius of Loyola puts it another way:

Prayer for Generosity

Lord, teach me to be generous.

Teach me to serve you as you deserve;

to give and not to count the cost,

to fight and not to heed the wounds, to toil and not to seek for rest,

to labor and not to ask for reward,

save that of knowing that I do your will.

—St. Ignatius of Loyola

Self can seem to keep getting in the way of all our relationships, yet I can discover via meditation that I am not the center of the universe. As Rick Warren points out in the first chapter of *The Purpose Driven Life*, it's not about me. My number-one purpose is to give God greater glory. As I mentioned earlier, sometimes when I am meditating, I will spontaneously find myself simply thanking God for each individual breath. Talk about getting back to basics. In other words, mindfulness helps me loosen my preoccupation with self and see and experience the bigger picture.

The prophets and saints have been teaching us this for

millennia, if we can just come to listen. St Francis of Assisi turned his back on a life of luxury as a wealthy European merchant like his father to live an austere life of selflessness and service to others. In sacrificing the self, he embraced God's call and experienced purpose and fulfillment. Men of his generation flocked to his fledgling order of friars because he exuded peace, joy, and freedom. This resulted from his decision to abandon worldly pursuits or achievements and devote his energy to benefiting others as he followed God's command to "rebuild my church." His philosophy was captured well in the now-famous Prayer of St. Francis in which he wrote, "O Divine Master, grant that I may not so much seek to be consoled as to console; to be understood as to understand; to be loved as to love." We must keep in mind that marriage is just as legitimate a vocation and opportunity for growth as being a Franciscan monk. Furthermore, meditating on Holy Scripture creates many opportunities to advance our understanding and patience with our spouse, and I highly recommend it. We all realize that our marriages would benefit enormously from affording greater patience toward our spouses.

Reflecting on the life of Joseph from the Old Testament, for instance, could serve as an inspiration. Joseph demonstrated tremendous patience in enduring a decade or two of estrangement from his family before reconciliation occurred with his eleven brothers. Now, I know myself. I have a hard time waiting fourteen days, sometimes, let alone fourteen years! How did Joseph do it? He trusted in God completely even when he was in the dungeons of the Pharaoh's palace!

Recognizing your inherent value and that of your

spouse likewise forges greater appreciation and can melt away divisiveness. Isaiah 43:4 asserts, "[Y]ou are precious in my eyes" and "I love you" (NABRE). Me? Precious to God? After all I've done? The answer is clearly yes and is testified by God's decision to ransom the life of His only son so I can share life in heaven for eternity. Likewise, it states in Psalm 139, "I can never be lost to your spirit! I can never get away from my God!" and "You are thinking of me constantly! … and when I waken in the morning, you are still thinking of me!" (Psalm 139:6, 17, 18 CLB). By word and example, meditating on God's word can foster greater understanding toward one's spouse and appreciation for his or her uniqueness. This idea was captured beautifully in the song "Fingerprints of God" by Steve Curtis Chapman. He wrote, "Never has there been and never again will there be another you. Fashioned by God's hand and perfectly planned to be just who you are. And what he's been creating since the first beat of your heart is a living, breathing priceless work of art." We pray that God will open our eyes to see our spouse with the fondness with which Christ sees him or her.

Marital expert Dr. John Gottman prescribes that spouses practice fondness. As difficult an assignment as this can be at times in our marriage, it absolutely works. Try it! Each day this week, write down one positive, endearing, or valued quality of your spouse. By week's end, not only will your attitude be improved toward your spouse, but your marriage will be more resilient.

> By simply reminding yourself of your spouse's positive qualities—even as you grapple with each other's flaws—you can prevent a happy marriage

from deteriorating. The simple reason is that fondness and admiration are antidotes for contempt. If you maintain a sense of respect for your spouse, you are less likely to act disgusted with him or her when you disagree. (Gottman, *The Seven Principles for Making Marriage Work, p.65*).

Understanding and appreciating our differences in personality, wiring, perception, and so on may be the most important first step toward strengthening one's marriage. This is what the late marital researcher Neil Jacobsen referred to as "acceptance work." If we are to live in one accord, as we are urged to do in the New Testament, we need to learn nonjudgment. Practicing mindfulness daily teaches us how to reserve judgment in our relationships verses pathologizing our differences. In fact, I believe my wife, Kathleen, and I make better decisions as a couple than we would as individuals *because* of our differences. She may get annoyed with me for being ponderous and indecisive when choosing what to order at a restaurant. I may get annoyed with her for making snap judgments when sizing up a new house. However, the truth is we bring different gifts to the marriage. Our personalities are almost completely opposite. However, Jungian expert Isabel Briggs Myers argues in her book *Gifts Differing* that people can be at opposite ends of the continuum on a given personality dimension and be quite compatible, as these are normal variations. So we say, "Viva la difference!"

I praise you because I am fearfully and wonderfully made; your works are wonderful, I know that full well.
—Psalm 139:14 (NIV)

Mindfulness Exercise #3

Interpersonal Effectiveness

I want each spouse to spend a moment jotting down his or her individual response to the following questions:

A. Recall the very first time you met and actually spoke to one another. What were the first things that attracted you to your spouse after that first meeting?

1. _____

2. _____

3. _____

B. Recall when you asked your spouse to marry you. What were the qualities in your mate that made you think, *Yes, I want to spend the rest of my life with this person*?

1. _____

2. _____

3. _____

C. When we first started going out, my favorite date was

_____

D. The reason it was so meaningful to me or enjoyable was

_____

_____

_____

After completing the journaling on your own, sit down together to share your responses to the questions. This is an opportunity to apply your mindful listening skills with your spouse. In other words, choose to simply listen to your spouse's ideas and opinions without questioning the content. Rather, practice giving him or her your full attention in terms of body posture and eye contact. You may choose to reflect back what you heard but avoid any judgment-laden remarks. Just keep it simple and light as you just listen and learn more about your spouse and some of the reasons he or she fell in love with you in the first place.

CHAPTER 4

Transforming Swords into Plowshares

Understanding the Nature of Conflict

Every couple I have ever seen in marital treatment has one complaint in common: communication. "We can't talk without fighting." "He never listens to me!" "She just doesn't get it!" "Sometimes, I feel like we are speaking different languages." "It's no use, we just can't communicate." Despite the ubiquitous nature of this goal, every experienced couple's counselor knows you never begin treatment with communication training. Most of us learned the hard way that typically this only prepares each partner to express in exquisite detail how miserable it is to live with his or her spouse! (This is why communication is reserved for a later chapter.)

Ideally, I begin marital treatment (after intake, history, rationale, treatment plan) with getting both partners to *act* differently toward each other. Often, they have been stuck in the same pattern of conflict for so long they can't see any other way to respond. In other words, they've been doing the foxtrot so long they forgot how to do the polka or the samba. Convincing clients to do something different is not easy. It is a big leap of faith for them because often so much resentment has built up they naturally assume the worst with every interaction. Motivation and attraction are at an all-time low point. One of the greatest psychotherapy trainers, Bill O'Hanlon, will direct his conflicted couples to have a fight the same day as their therapy appointment but change one aspect of it. For example, he might suggest, "I want you to have the same fight tonight after dinner as usually happens, but instead of having it in the kitchen, as you typically do, I want you to have it in the garage" or "fight about the same topic at eight tonight in the kitchen, but instead of both standing at the island counter, I want John to sit cross-legged on the kitchen floor, and, Sue, I want you to hop up and sit on the island throughout the course of the argument." It is fascinating how changing one action can disrupt a rigid pattern of conflict and give them a significantly different perspective or, perhaps, enable them to learn an entirely new dance!

Dealing with Our Humanness

Part of the challenge in resolving conflict is that the human brain is hardwired for remembering bad stuff. Over the eons, this was critical for survival of the species. Put another way, if a distant ancestor was to miss noticing a lovely piece of fruit on his or her travels, he or she would live to procreate. However, if that same person missed noticing the saber-toothed tiger … You get the picture. Our brains function the same way within our marital relationships. I may not notice that my wife ironed my favorite shirt or was kind when I got a speeding ticket the week before, but I may remember how hurt I felt after our last fight. In fact, I remember every word, scowl, and reaction in vivid detail. Although I may not be able to change my biology, mindfulness can help me respond differently in the face of conflict. It can teach me to notice and acknowledge my ineffective tendencies and to create space between my thoughts and emotions and actions so I don't just "go off," and it can assist in my becoming aware of my blind spots. Blind spots are negative or unhealthy tendencies that I am unaware of yet others may notice. As Victor Frankl stated in *Man's Search for Meaning*, "Between stimulus and response, there is a space. In that space is our power to choose our response. In our response lies our growth and our freedom."

Some spouses will experience what author and psychologist Martin Seligman coined "learned helplessness." In the late 1960s, Seligman was working as an experimental psychologist in an animal laboratory. They had developed a two-sided dog cage with wire mesh on the floor of each side that could alternatively omit a low-voltage shock to the animal. The experimenters were studying the relationship between fear and learning. They would flip on the electricity on one side of the cage and measure how fast the dog would leap over the abbreviated fence inside the cage to the other side. One day, Seligman wondered in the midst of the experiment what would happen if he flipped the voltage on both sides simultaneously. What he observed was that the dog would try jumping over to the other side to escape the pain only to discover the same problem on the other side. After a few attempts to try the other side of the cage, the canine would simply lie down and take it. Even when he saw the researcher shut off the other side, the dog just lay there and took the shock, looking sad and lethargic. Seligman coined the term *learned helplessness* as a theory to explain depression. However, the same phenomenon can be observed in couples with troubled marriages. Their anticipated future is based on failures of the past to the point that even when one partner is making positive strides to be a more loving husband or wife, the other partner remains cynical, listless, discouraged, or even hopeless.

To change the effect of learned helplessness on the laboratory dogs, Seligman and his colleagues had to apply the shock and coax or even drag the dog to the other side of the cage to realize there was hope and reverse the effects of the training. In marital treatment, I have to train the partner to "act first and the feelings will follow." This is why I sometimes recommend the book *Ten Great Dates to Energize Your Marriage* by David and Claudia Arp. The book outlines precisely where you will go, what you will do, and the topics you will talk about. Even though some couples are resistant at first, this constitutes one way to "rewrite your love story and rediscover the simple joys of shared engagement and quality time. You are learning to focus on the present activity, a key principle of mindfulness. The discipline of mindfulness is an antidote to learned helplessness because it teaches us to focus on one thing and redirect our attention to the present and allows us to practice seeing moment to moment experiences as workable. As when we practice the breath meditation, rather than judging a given breath as good or bad, smooth or difficult, we accept it for what it is, its own unique experience.

The most common way I demonstrate the application of mindfulness to marriage is via the bubble exercise. I simply purchase a small bottle of children's bubbles, blow some bubbles in the office, and instruct each person to pick out one bubble, focus exclusively on the qualities of that single bubble, and see what he or she notices. We then discuss what we observed, such as the size, colors, movement, shape, and perhaps feel (if it landed on one's arm) or even the sound when it popped. I explain that blowing bubbles is typically an intrinsic exercise in mindfulness because I am focusing on one thing (a single bubble), staying in the moment (not thinking about past experiences with bubbles or future opportunities to blow bubbles), and reserving judgment (not saying my bubble should not have popped so quickly or determining this to be a good activity or not).

Inner Resources to Adapt Our Reactions

By this point, I may begin to get some looks of curiosity as to how this relates to marital conflict. I explain that the biggest problem that causes or perpetuates our arguments is that we react to each other's reactions, or, as I sometimes say, "I am codependent to my wife's codependency." For example, let's say a husband does something thoughtless and his wife says, "Jim, you are such a selfish bastard!" Now, I don't know about you, but I know that my typical reaction in this sort of situation would be to either get defensive ("Hey! You could do a lot worse than me!"), lash out with a counterattack ("You know what your problem is? You always have to criticize every little thing I do!), or withdraw (pull away into sullen quietude and pout). None of these reactions are particularly helpful in an ongoing relationship.

However, if he were to treat her words like a bubble in the room, he could respond mindfully to a challenging situation. Much like the bubble, her comment has a size, shape, color, intensity, and so on. Rather than just reacting, he can draw from his past experience with mindfulness meditation by focusing on one thing (this conversation), staying in the moment (not drudging up old hurtful comments from years past or assuming it will always be this way), and reserving judgment (not automatically evaluating this as a bad moment).

It may be tempting to ignore the speaker. "La la la la la, I'm not listening to this!" Alternatively, one might think, *I am just an awful, worthless person*, like her words were an indictment handed down on a stone tablet by God. The beauty of routinely practicing mindfulness meditation is it can prepare me to respond to her comment about being a selfish bastard as if it were simply an idea to be considered, as merely one person's opinion not to be assumed true or ignored. If Jim were to pause without reacting and consider her words at face value, he may conclude two things: 1) technically, I am not a bastard because I know who my parents were, and 2) truth be told, I can be very selfish at times. Recall in Proverbs 9:7–9, it suggests "the wise man welcomes admonishment, the fool rejects correction." A few seconds of mindfulness in the midst of the storm could allow him to respond meaningfully to her. "You know what, honey? You are right. I have been very selfish at times in our marriage, and I am sorry. I know I have hurt you because of my selfishness, and I hope you will forgive me." Notice that Jim is not agreeing with the pejorative application of the word "bastard," which may have been just a projection of her hurt, but paused to seek out the truth in her opinion regarding his selfishness and, therefore, could validate her feelings. Furthermore, we know from Proverbs 15:1 (NIV) that "a gentle answer turns away wrath, but a harsh word stirs up anger."

Our initial reactions during a fight are often reflections of past hurts that may predate even meeting one's spouse. Other times, our impulse is to fly into the future filled with fear that the anger we are witnessing in this moment will be unremitting, and we imagine ourselves miserably enduring constant attacks for years to come.

Canadian psychologist and marital expert Dr. Sue Johnson explained it this way in an excerpt from her book *Hold Me Tight*:

> To reconnect, lovers have to be able to de-escalate the conflict and actively create a basic emotional safety. They need to be able to work in concert to curtail their negative dialogues and to defuse their fundamental insecurities. They may not be as close as they crave to be, but they can now step on each other's toes and then turn and do damage control. They can have their own differences and not careen helplessly into Demon Dialogues. They can rub each other's raw spots and not slide into anxious demands or numbing withdrawal. They can deal better with the disorienting ambiguity that their loved one, who is the solution to fear, can also suddenly become a source of fear.

To summarize, by focusing on creating a sense of emotional safety for one's spouse, it enables the couple to maintain better emotional balance. This establishes a solid base upon which spouses can begin to do repairs of relational rifts. Bringing mindfulness into our marriage fosters the emotional balance Johnson referred to in the preceding excerpt. Treating harsh verbal attacks like a bubble in the room opens the gap between affect and action, which can create space within to consider meaningful options versus lashing back with anger or contempt. In other words, we can focus on *what* rather than *why*. Like an athlete who is "in the zone," we experience the flow of relational awareness in the moment versus what happened earlier in the game or worrying about the final score.

Opportunities to Grow

Married couples often fight over who is right and who is wrong. One spouse thinks the other is too hard on the kids while the other believes his or her spouse is too permissive. One feels the in-laws are too involved in their lives; the other sees it as a huge blessing or views it as support. One argues for an economy car, the other an SUV. Ironically, if you win the battle, you lose the war. In other words, if I hammer home my perspective and convince my wife she's totally off base, she feels defeated, even demeaned, and the main objective (closeness, trust, safety, valuing) is lost. If you want to ensure greater distance and animosity, ensure you win every argument. It is important to recognize, as mentioned in chapter 3, we bring different gifts to the marriage as a result of our experiences, personalities, and unique perspectives. If we can strive to be mindful listeners and remain open to influence, we are likely to arrive at better solutions than we would on our own.

One spouse may shine a light on his or her shadow self. My wife is very alert to my blind spots—character flaws I am not aware of that are obvious to her. If I am receptive to feedback, I can grow and become a better husband and father. Practicing mindfulness meditation can help me be open versus defensive or attacking, as I am not judging these conflicted conversations as bad. Interestingly, anger can be a pathway to marital intimacy. Likewise, problems can either drive us apart or draw us closer together. Let me share an example of this phenomenon.

Justin and Esther were a beautiful example of how the manure of life can cause the garden of a marital relationship to grow. Justin and Esther had two children. I first met them when their nineteen-year-old son died suddenly from a rare heart defect. They were utterly devastated. As the weeks passed, Esther confided that she was just biding her time until she would die. She needed Justin's support and a listening ear, but he was like a zombie just going through the motions of each day. I had several sessions of counseling with their fifteen-year-old daughter, who suffered from depression now compounded by the grief of losing her older brother, whom she adored, as he was the one person who could make her laugh. Less than two years later, the daughter died of the same undetectable heart condition. My heart broke for Justin and Esther. I'd known other couples whose marriage imploded following the death of a child because of blaming one another, complete withdrawal from the family or pathologizing the other's way of grieving as too much or not enough. I feared for their marital viability after they buried their second child. To my surprise, they did much better over the months following the second loss. I attributed this to three factors: 1) they took great solace in their faith that their children were together in heaven, 2) we had done some work on mindfulness prior to the second loss, and 3) they decided to lean on one another for emotional support. Rather than driving them apart, the tragedy brought them closer together despite their different personalities and grieving styles.

Christians often wonder why a loving God would allow good people to suffer. Although I have read several good essays and books on this topic, one of the most compelling answers to the question of suffering is that God fully realizes these are tremendous opportunities for us to grow. Suffering may lead us to grow closer to one another as in the case of Justin and Esther. Personal experience with pain or trauma can foster greater compassion and understanding for those experiencing loss or troubles currently. Research by clinical psychologist Dr. Robert Brooks and others has demonstrated that if we can view adversity, disappointments, and setbacks as opportunities to learn and grow versus personal failures, we will grow in resilience. This certainly has relevance for marital success. Probably the most powerful reason God would permit suffering in the lives of the ones He loves is it can result in greater reliance on and closeness to Christ. For many in modern society believe if everything is going fine, who needs God? It is in my pain and struggle that I realize how desperately I need a savior in my life. Left to my own devices, I tend to make a mess of things, including my marriage. Likewise, conflict in our marital relationship is best viewed as an opportunity to grow interpersonally and in relationship to God.

Mindfulness Exercise #4

The Apple Meditation

The apple meditation is simply an eating meditation in which you spend a minimum of ten minutes eating a single apple. Be conscious of the appearance. Avoid as many external distractions as is reasonable so as to give it your full attention. Notice the sound of the crunch with each bite. Experience how the texture changes as you slowly savor each bite. Strive to stay in the present moment by not comparing it to other apples you have eaten. Reserve judgment as to whether you like apples or not, and simply observe your moment-to-moment experience. See if you can experience the extraordinary in the ordinary.

> For I know the plans I have for you, says the
> Lord. They are plans for good and not for
> evil, to give you a future and a hope.
> —Jeremiah 29:11 (The Living Bible)

Chapter 5

Betrayal and Trust

Cultivating Good Soil

Just as high-quality soil is the foundation for a healthy garden, trust and security form the foundation for a growing marriage. When my wife knows I love her and senses that I want to be with her and only her, it is like having deep, rich, loamy soil that the plant can sink its roots into forming a strong base for the plant or tree to grow. However, too often, my selfish preoccupation with looking out for my interests and needs over hers ruins the soil conditions. It is like having an inch of soil with rocks below. Good things can sprout but seldom last, and the little saplings are sure to get knocked over with the next strong wind.

Dave and Theresa were married about fourteen years when they first came to see me. They had three young boys, and Dave was very successful in his line of work. I could tell they were upset the moment they sat down in my office. Theresa was tearful, and Dave appeared numb as they shared how Dave had had an affair with a woman from work. Theresa was hurt and angry. Dave was stoic and asked how one does an amicable divorce. I continued to do my initial couples evaluation but fortunately was not completely clear about their intentions to split up. So I asked Dave point-blank if he really wanted to end his marriage to Theresa. He said, "Actually, no. I love Theresa and would prefer to stay together, but I figure it's hopeless and she'll never be able to forgive me so why bother?" I asked Theresa the same question, and she responded that she loved Dave and wanted to work things out and remain together. It was clear that the trust was demolished, but Dave went from emotionless to tearful when Theresa professed she still very much loved him.

The emotional impact of betrayal can be devastating. Inadequacy, fear, anger, and hurt are common reactions. Too many times, I have been face to face with a new therapy couple in which the husband or wife or, in some cases, both acknowledged infidelity, and both are distraught. Both may be crying, disillusioned, and can't imagine how they will ever recover or be able to trust each other again. Instilling hope becomes critical because the father of lies would love the Christian couple in this predicament to believe reconciliation is hopeless.

The first step on the road to recovery is to stop the bleeding by cutting all ties with the third party complicit in the affair. The second step is to willingly become completely transparent by handing over your phone and computer passwords. The next step is to ask forgiveness and begin to make amends. Mindfulness is instrumental at this stage because it can allow one to express contrition by owning what one did without getting defensive, blaming one's partner, or making excuses. Healing and forgiveness take time and patience. Here again mindfulness can be pivotal, as healing requires great forbearance.

Nearly every spouse attempting to recover from an affair echoes the same perspective. The infidel suggests they have to find a way to put the affair behind them, start afresh, and move on. The betrayed partner says, "Hold on—no way? We have to look back so we understand how we got into this mess in the first place!"

I look at the couple squarely and say, "You are both absolutely correct!" We do need to find a way to put the past in the past so to mindfully embrace the present. God gives us here and now as a platform upon which we can build a brighter future together. However, we also need to look within and examine the past to discover the beliefs, decisions, and justifications that led up to the affair. Otherwise, what is to prevent him or her from the same mistakes five years from now? Returning to the garden metaphor, the last thing you want to do is step on the same tomato plant again. I often reassure them that the plant can make a full recovery, but it will likely take months rather than days so patience is essential.

Compassion Promotes Healing

How long it takes the heart to heal and begin to trust again is difficult to predict. This begs the question, how does one tolerate the discomfort of the hurt and distrust while the heart slowly mends? Mindfulness has much to offer in this respect. For the one who caused the hurt, mindfulness practice prepares him or her to do two things:

1. acknowledge responsibility while genuinely seeking forgiveness without continuously beating him- or herself up for his or her mistakes; 2. not assuming that just because the other partner is extremely hurt and angry today that it will always be that way in the future but rather take it day by day. This may also allow the unfaithful partner to take solace in God's mercy, such as envisioning the Father running down the road to embrace the prodigal son and celebrate his homecoming. For the one who was betrayed, the challenge becomes how to move beyond continually dwelling on the images of what she or he imagined happened. In addition, how does the one who was hurt stop living in fear of another betrayal? Mindfulness is not designed to escape thoughts or feelings. Rather, it can help us be more fully in the present while acknowledging the memories of the past or doubts about the future may still linger as with the death of a loved one.

Restoring trust takes time and patience. I often encourage the one who was cheated on to transition his or her trust from the spouse to Christ Jesus. In other words, when he or she can't seem to trust the spouse because the wound is too raw, he or she can make a conscious decision to place trust in the Lord (who will never ever betray him or her) until he or she is able to begin trusting the spouse again.

Infidelity can do serious damage to one's self-esteem, confidence, and self-image. Many who are betrayed feel terribly vulnerable and inadequate. They often blame themselves and assume they are not good enough. A decent proportion of these survivors suffer from PTSD. Practicing mindfulness meditation can contribute significantly to one's recovery. As one becomes more experienced in mindfulness meditation, one discovers the ability to acknowledge, observe, and honor emotions rather than assume these negative feelings are a reflection of one's worth. With mindfulness, we can treat these difficult emotions as an unexpected guest and discover compassion for ourselves. In a similar vein, I will often encourage someone struggling with low self-worth to meditate on Psalm 139. Herein we find one of several excellent scriptural messages indicating how precious you are to God. Sitting with this passage and giving it our full attention, we allow this truth to sink into the depths of our soul.

Mindfulness Exercise #5

Faith Walk

The faith walk is the first mindfulness exercise you will try as a couple. Find a thick scarf or something you can use as a blindfold. Flip a coin to see who gets to go first. Put on the blindfold so you cannot see anything. The spouse who is the leader may not speak at all during the exercise, but the blindfolded spouse can speak freely. The leader takes his or her spouse by the hand or arm and guides him or her on a ten-minute walk through the house or hike through the woods. The leader can use nonverbal cues to the blindfolded follower as to changes in terrain, such as tapping the follower's knee to alert him or her of a stair or an obstacle. Spinning the person slowly around once or twice can be a little disorienting but forces the blindfolded spouse to rely more on the leader. Be patient and gentle as the leader, but make it fun or interesting by taking the person's hand to touch a leaf or a tree or the family dog. After ten minutes, switch roles. Afterward, it can be intriguing to discuss what each noticed both as leader and follower. We rely heavily on our vision to guide our movements, yet when blindfolded, we intuitively begin to have a heightened awareness of sounds and the somatosensory elements of touch. It also can lead to a discussion about whom we trust and how easy or difficult it can be to trust another not to walk us into a wall! Sharing about what the leader did to safely guide the follower along without the benefit of sight helps us to begin understanding in a simple, practical way how we can create an atmosphere of emotional safety.

He heals the broken-hearted and bandages their wounds.
　—Psalm 147:3 (Good News Third Edition [GNTD])

The Lord is near to those who are discouraged:
　he saves those who have lost all hope.
　　　—Psalm 34:18 (GNTD)

CHAPTER 6

Parenting

The Most Important Job in the World

Couples who are blessed to have children discover this can create a number of common challenges to their marital relationship. Each spouse may come into marriage with a different philosophy regarding child rearing. For example, one spouse may feel that children are like flowers and if given the proper space and soil conditions will naturally flourish. The other spouse, however, may believe that children need a great deal of structure and guidance, or they will falter and go down the wrong path. With five kids, it was often nearly impossible to find quiet time for just the two of us to nurture our relationship. With the shopping, giving baths, school projects, meals, extracurricular activities, and so on, we were lucky to have ten minutes to talk some days. Dates were so much work to arrange, we questioned whether it was even worth it. Some kids cling to Mom, some talk back to Dad, some are painfully shy, and another isolates or is rebellious. This is not to mention the challenge of having a special needs child or ailing parents in your family and the time and energy it takes to meet their needs. So exactly how can a married couple work effectively as a team, adequately respond to the unique personality of each child, and still have quality time together? Mindfulness.

I recall a pivotal day in our marriage when we had bought our first house and had our second child. It was about ten at night, and I was reading the paper in the living room when I heard a muted sound coming from the kitchen. I glanced into the kitchen and realized Kathleen was softly weeping while washing dishes at the kitchen sink. I got up, went into the kitchen, and asked, "Are you okay? Do you want my help?"

She replied flatly but resolutely, "No, Ted, I don't want your help."

For the past few years, the demands on her time with two little ones and the sheer number of household tasks had multiplied. However, when she'd ask for my help in the evenings, I would complain how tired I was and appear so put out by even the simplest request, she gave up and closed down. For the next week or two, it didn't matter how nicely I offered to help, she was not having it. Her heart had closed down because I neglected to recognize and respond to her growing need for help with the kids and the house.

A big part of the problem was me. I had come into marriage with a template based on my parents' division of roles and responsibilities. My father worked long hours at the butcher shop, and when he got home, he would put his feet up on the couch, do the bills for the shop, and fall asleep watching *Wild Kingdom*. Subconsciously, I thought my role was to work at the hospital and rest at home. Fortunately,

I persisted in offering to help Kathleen in the evenings, and in time, her heart softened, and we began to work more as a team. Ironically, I trained my chronic pain clients in mindfulness every day partly to foster greater present moment awareness, but I failed to practice that awareness at home until I had this epiphany. Now when I do the dishes, I use it as an opportunity to practice mindfulness meditation.

Have you ever played the game Candyland? If you haven't, let me forewarn you. It is a mind-numbingly simple game for adults. However, young children love it, as it only requires you to know your primary colors. I recall playing this board game with my own children when they were about four to six years old. I would turn over a card, and it would show blue, for instance. As I am moving my gingerbread man to the first blue square on the candy trail, I would be thinking, *As soon as I am done with this silly game, I need to go out to the garage and see if I still have that can of white paint* ... Before I know it, I look up and realize they've already gone, and it is my turn again. This could go on for most of the game. I'm here, but I'm not *really* here. Other times, I can get easily annoyed. My kids are competitive. They will fight each other over who gets the blue versus the green gingerbread man before we even begin to play the game! I would get aggravated and exclaim, "Can we just play the game? Take my game piece. I don't care what color I get!"

However, when I am able to incorporate mindfulness into these everyday interactions, I notice some interesting differences. I am able to be more responsive than reactive. I am emotionally available to my wife and children rather than checked out or self-absorbed. And even if they're fighting,

I handle it more gracefully. If they are fighting during the game, I might consider, *Michael John was up kind of late last night. Maybe he's just tired, and that's why he's melting down. I haven't spent much time with Mary Grace today. Maybe she is just craving some normal attention from Dad. Maybe this is a chance to teach them something about conflict resolution.* It can be a lot of things if I am here … but so often I'm not. Too often, our minds are preoccupied with other things, and the inherent challenges of raising children elicit frustration or withdrawal. Yet Psalm 127 reads, "Children are a gift from the LORD; they are a reward from him" (NLT).

Honing my mindfulness skills and awareness helped transform me from angry and exasperated to patient and consistent as a father. I have always admired Mother Theresa of Calcutta and the patience and generosity with which she mindfully cared for the indigent children and elderly of India. It calls to mind two of my favorite Mother Theresa quotes that relate to parenting mindfully: "Saying there are too many children in the world is like saying there are too many flowers" and "I may not be able to do great things, but I can do little things with great love." She recognized that each and every child is a gift from God to the world. It is a gift to be able to move from judging their quirky little habits to appreciating their funny expressions, their creative ideas, and the wonder in their eyes. Caring for and disciplining children requires a lot of time and energy. Simple tasks, such as getting their shoes and coats on, takes them more time than they do adults. We could just do these tasks for them for the sake of expediency, or we could start getting ready a little sooner, allow them to do them, and celebrate their successes. One of my greatest regrets is that, due to my perfectionism, I ruined the experience of gardening with my kids when they were little. I would redo each row and make sure every seed was evenly spaced. I wish I could go back in time, give them a corner of the garden, and just say, "Have fun!" and let them plant whatever they wanted, however they wanted, and see what came up—hence the expression "do little things with great love."

The other lesson from Mother Theresa was her wisdom in understanding the significance of a simple smile. When training novices in her order, she emphasized the healing power of a smile with every child or patient they would serve. I was infamous among my children for the "Ted-look." If I got cut off in traffic, I would give the person a look of complete disgust and disapproval. It happened so often my kids would ask, "Dad, did you just give that guy the Ted-look?" I was unaware how often I wore that face around the house until my wife challenged me to look in the mirror because I looked like I wanted to kill someone. At first, I said she was crazy and that was just the face God gave me. But in time I took her advice and looked in the mirror periodically over the course of a typical weekend at home. Let's just say the look was anything but warm and inviting. So I became more mindful of my countenance and practiced smiling more. In addition to managing our own personal reactions to our children, we must also contend with our spouse's parenting strategies, which may be very different from our own.

Differing Gifts

Bringing home your newborn infant from the hospital is a special moment for any parent. Most experience an amalgam of excitement, nervousness, and awe. Unfortunately, they don't send you home with a parenting manual that tells you what to do when your three-year-old draws a mural on your dining room wall with permanent marker, your ten-year-old discovers pornography on the internet, or your sixteen-year-old gets dumped by a boyfriend or girlfriend. Parenting requires a great deal of wisdom. For better or worse, we all come into marriage with preconceived notions and expectations regarding child rearing based on our own primary family experiences. Different rules, privileges, ways to regulate emotions, and styles of discipline were modeled for us by our parents. The first time your two-year-old steals a cookie from the jar, you and your spouse may well be confronted with two very different expectations on how it should be handled. One may say, "If I took a cookie without asking, I got paddled." The other may suggest, "We were allowed to eat anything in the house at any time as long as we ate our supper." I've never met a couple with children who have never fought over child-rearing ideas and practices.

God intended children to be raised by a father and a mother because we each bring unique ingredients to the recipe of how to raise healthy kids of good character. A father often brings toughness, resilience, a sense of adventure, and a willingness to take risks to the mix. A mother often contributes gentleness and compassion, along with stressing the importance of relationships and manners.

This is not to suggest that women are not competitive and men can't model gentleness. It is highlighting how we bring very different qualities to the family. Practicing mindfulness meditation daily cultivates a listening heart, which is so vital to effective parenting. If we are not so quick to judge or dismiss alternative viewpoints on handling the kids, we often arrive at a synthesis, hybrid, or balanced approach to parenting.

I can recall when the kids were small and I was trying to clean the kitchen. Inevitably, one of them would come up, tug on my pant leg, and ask me to come play. I responded with "I'll play with you in ten minutes when I'm done in the kitchen."

Two minutes later, he returns. "Daddy, please come play."

Irritated, I say, "Quit bothering me. I'll play when I'm done."

Two minutes later, my son says, "Daddy! When are you gonna be done?"

I lose my temper and yell, "Would you stop it?"

Now my wife could be in the same position and want to get the kitchen done just as much but handle it completely differently. She would think about her options and respond relationally. She'd say, "Okay, let's play." She would give him her undivided attention for ten minutes, and he would be content for the next two hours. Kathleen always recognized that time with the children is a precious and fleeting opportunity because they grow up so fast. In the book *The Sixty Minute Father*, Rob Parsons states that, for kids, love is spelled "T-I-M-E."

The Many Benefits of Mindful Parenting

Mindfulness is the manifestation of quality time and the antidote to a plethora of pediatric and adolescent problems. Parental interest and involvement in their child's education is strongly correlated with academic success. Teens who have an involved father are significantly less likely to drop out or fail high school. Boys raised without a physically or emotionally engaged father are significantly more likely to end up in prison. Girls raised without their dad in the house are more likely to experience an unplanned pregnancy.

Mindfulness training is a gift to the bored father or unfulfilled mother. Time drifts by as they go through the motions of marriage, work, and family. If they could view parenting as an adventure, like a mountain to be climbed, they could experience greater engagement. This is a blessing to both the child and the parent. Likewise, eliciting participation of the children in a challenge both the parent and the child find inspiring is a huge opportunity to connect and build self-esteem. Examples of shared activities could include carpentry, music, service projects, cross-country skiing, painting, cooking, and so on. Hiking has always been a way to connect with my children, especially when we'd go off trail and have to traverse a gorge or cross a stream. It is a chance to reinforce their courage, creativity, and perseverance. We would pretend we were Lewis and Clark exploring the untamed wilderness of the West and had to use our wits to overcome unforeseen obstacles. We would make forts out of fallen trees and branches. We would use rocks to create bridges over rushing creeks. Typically, when we would be deep into one of our hikes, my wife or

I would have all five of our children stop and be quiet and still for one full minute to listen and use their other senses to simply observe what they noticed. Afterward we'd ask what they noticed. They would comment on the sound of a bird chirping, the feel of the breeze upon their faces, the smell of the pine trees wafting through the air. They didn't realize it, but we were teaching them to appreciate the wonder of God's creativity through a simple mindfulness exercise.

My wife would sometimes question whether her efforts to parent mindfully were really making a difference. She would see her peers in seemingly important careers and would wonder if she had missed the boat. I would remind her that her being a stay-at-home mom was the most important job in the world. It was not just a blessing to our children, but healthy, strong families are the foundation of a healthy society.

In their book *Raising Great Kids*, Cloud and Townsend suggest that just as children are taught the "3 Rs" in school of "reading, 'riting, and 'rithmatic," parents need to teach the 3 Rs of respect, responsibility, and resourcefulness. Mindfulness affords us the opportunity to tag them as parents. If I am aware my wife's nerves are wearing thin after a long day with the kids, I can offer to step in and provide the structure and guidance needed without yelling. Kids don't come into this world knowing how to demonstrate respect; it must be taught, reinforced, and role-modeled. I recommend if a child is disrespectful, such as talking back to his or her mother, that the father intervenes and vice versa. This avoids a lot of yelling, arguing, and debating involved in trying to get that child to respect you. Rather, as the dad, I might say, "Hold on, young man. She is not just your mother; she is also my wife, and I expect you to treat her with respect. Is that clear?" There is no yelling and no pleading, but there may well be mention of a consequence if I hear the same tone or attitude in the future.

One of the greatest challenges for parents is disciplining out of love and not out of anger. We often intervene and confront problem behavior because it upsets us. However, I am sending a mixed message if I threaten and yell while I am trying to teach respect. My daily meditation practice has significantly helped me to stay in the moment with the immediate behavioral issue while remaining mindful of the overarching goal of character development. By not judging the interaction as good or bad, I am able to respond in a calm and focused manner. This creates a more peaceful family atmosphere in which the kids know Mom and Dad are in charge of their well-being without nagging, belittling, or shaming them.

With our busy lifestyles and active families, it can be difficult to find quiet time to establish a mindfulness meditation practice. Although devoting time to prayer and meditation involves a sacrifice of time, it is an investment in your personal well-being and the health of your relationships. Even though it requires time on the front end, we are rewarded with greater productivity and emotional intelligence over the course of time. The final benefit of mindfulness to parenting is the realization that I now have unlimited time to myself. In other words, when I'm playing catch with my son, it is *my* time with my son. When I am checking my daughter's essay, it is my time with my daughter. When I am discussing bills with my wife, it is my time with my wife. To summarize, mindfulness has helped me become a more effective and engaged parent.

Mindfulness Exercise #6

Body Scan

Find a quiet place to sit or lie down. Begin by focusing your attention, as best you can, on the big toe of your left foot. Does it feel big or small? Cool or warm? Simply notice any sensations for fifteen to twenty seconds without judging these feelings as good or bad. Between your big toe and the next is a little space. What are the sensations there? If you were to gently wiggle your toes, you may notice a subtle experience of friction. Take a few moments to notice what that is like. Guide your awareness up to the instep or top of your feet where your shoelaces would typically be if wearing shoes. You may become aware of the gentle pressure or sense of containment from the tongue of your shoe upon the top of your foot. What are the sensations at these places of contact? After a while, glide your attention to the sole or arch of your feet. Do the bottoms of your feet feel smooth or rough, moist or dry? However they feel is how they feel at this moment. Just notice what you are noticing without any need to explain or change it. Rather, simply experience the various sensations with an attitude of gentleness and curiosity. Bringing your awareness to your ankles, take fifteen or twenty seconds to notice if these joints feel tired or strong or tense or relaxed.

As you can see from the preceding sample, one would systematically pause to notice the sensations in one's own body without evaluating those experiences as positive or negative. Once you have gotten through the feet and ankles, you bring the same present-moment awareness to the remaining segments of the body: shins, calves, knees, thighs, hips, stomach, back, shoulders, arms, hands, neck, face, and scalp. Finally, I would spend a minute just noticing how the body feels as a whole and end by focusing on the breath for a minute or two.

> Fathers, do not aggravate your children,
> or they will become discouraged.
> —Colossians 3:21 (New Living Translation)

CHAPTER 7

Sexual Intimacy

God created each of us as sexual beings. Sex is a beautiful expression of love between a husband and a wife. Most dating or engaged couples can't wait to be married so they can finally be together sexually. So why does every marital expert rank sex in the top three or four most common topics couples fight about? There are numerous reasons why so many couples experience disconnect regarding sexual intimacy. Probably the most common reason is because men are microwaves and women are Crockpots.

When I first heard this expression years ago, I thought it was brilliant. I would guess it can occur in reverse for 10 to 15 percent of couples, but for the vast majority, it is true that men are microwaves. We could have no interaction with our wives for three or four days and like a cup of water in a microwave suddenly get heated up and be in the mood to make love. Our wives, in contrast, typically pull away and ask, "What are you doing? I haven't talked to you in days. I feel like I hardly know you!"

We husbands think, *What's up? Did I do something*

wrong? Why the cold shoulder? Did I say something insensitive or hurtful today? We are befuddled and often feel rejected or undesirable. What we fail to understand is that women are Crockpots. It is the quality time, kind gestures, and rich conversation over the course of the week that generate closeness and stimulate their sexual desire. Guys don't need all that buildup. However, research has demonstrated that husbands who have a close, engaging, and emotionally involved relationship with their wives outside of the bedroom rate their sex life significantly more satisfying than men who engage in casual hookups.

Without the closeness and positive interactions over the course of a day or two, making love feels out of context for women. They cannot relax and lend themselves openly to the sexual encounter unless they feel emotionally safe, which is a natural outcome of mindfulness-infused quality time. When we routinely check in with our wives regarding the state of their heart, they feel valued. I will periodically ask Kathleen, "Do you feel loved, honored, and cherished?" and "If not, what can I do to support you better?" Likewise, if there are laughter, playfulness, and shared activities, sex feels like it is a part of a larger context in a loving, committed relationship. She doesn't feel like she is merely a means to an end. To summarize, being fully present outside the bedroom creates a context for being fully present and engaged when in bed making love.

Take the case of Mike and Megan as an example. They were a nice Christian couple in their thirties with two young children. After the kids went to bed, Mike began smoking marijuana most evenings with his brother-in-law, who was living with them for several months. Later in the evening, he would go to bed and want to make love, but Megan wanted nothing to do with him. Mike would get perturbed as a result of her rejection and would tell her to "lighten up!" He would argue that the smoking was "no big deal, and besides I don't do it every night." She was clearly turned off by his marijuana use and told him it disgusted her. He would react to her negativity with more defensiveness and would counterattack with "You overreact to everything!" Megan had many fears regarding how his substance abuse could adversely affect them, including his physical health, their financial situation, and the potential negative influence on their children over the years. She may have attempted to communicate these concerns, but mostly what he experienced from her were angry verbal attacks and a withdrawal of affection and sexual intimacy. She needed to confront the truth in love, but her anger got in the way. Mike's preoccupation with his own comfort and pleasure kept him stuck in an unhealthy pattern that was draining the life out of their marriage. They did not realize that men are microwaves and women are Crockpots.

I began intensive training in mindfulness meditation with them and urged them to practice daily. Megan discovered that mindfulness helped her to respond to the problem assertively out of love rather than fear. In 2 Timothy 1:7 (NKJV), it says, "For God has not given us a spirit of fear; but of power, and of love, and of a sound mind." Mike was better able to listen to her concerns without getting defensive or sarcastic, and he found the meditation practice relaxing. He gave up the marijuana use and devoted this energy to more quality time with Megan, which, in turn, created a sense of presence and emotional safety for her.

She felt closer, and her desire for sexual intimacy returned, which was a healthy source of comfort for Mike.

St. Paul urges the Christian couples of Ephesus to "be submissive to one another." This includes patience regarding sex. If my wife has had a long day and is tired or doesn't feel well, the loving response would be, "That's okay, sweetheart. Perhaps we can be together tomorrow night," without making her feel guilty. Likewise, if I had a stressful day at work and have a strong desire for the comfort and release lovemaking provides, my wife is kind and understanding without making me feel like I am putting her out or ashamed of expressing a need. Mindfulness is well known to foster compassion. Compassion leads to this openness and responsivity. This is why the most important factor for the sexual satisfaction of your spouse is not your body but your mind. Your ability to listen and respond without judgment sets your husband or wife at ease to reveal what is pleasurable, respectful, comforting, or exciting. One person may be aroused more visually while another is tactilly. One spouse may find the scent of a particular cologne alluring while another may prefer auditory stimulation.

Routine practice of mindfulness meditation teaches us how to live in the moment. Remaining in the moment dramatically increases the likelihood of a satisfying sex life. If during lovemaking a husband is anxious about a meeting with his boss the next day or a wife is worried about their daughter getting into a certain college, they are not fully present to one another. Likewise, if a wife is recalling how she did not achieve orgasm the last time they were intimate or a husband is worried about maintaining an erection, they may be preoccupied with the final outcome rather than simply enjoying the present-moment sensations. Sometimes we are so stuck ruminating about some past hurt, argument, or betrayal that it pulls us away from being engaged in the here and now.

The key to remaining in the moment is mindfully experiencing sensations versus evaluating them. For example, if I were to start a fire in the fire pit in the backyard, I could judge the fire to be dangerous or, alternatively, I could observe, describe, and experience the quality of the flames—the colors, smells, and warmth emitted by the glowing embers. The couple I mentioned earlier, Mike and Megan, struggled initially to reconnect sexually so I suggested sensate focus.

Learning to Be in the Moment

Sensate focus is a process in which mindfulness is applied to sexual intimacy for couples having trouble in this department. For so many couples, the root of their sexual problems is spending too much time in their heads and not enough in their bodies. As stated before, we may be ruminating about the past or worried about our sexual performance or how it will turn out in the end. Basically, we overthink sex. I will sometimes have couples start by simply massaging their partner's hands and taking notice of what area, speed, or degree of pressure seems most pleasant or pleasing to their spouse. With sensate focus, I will encourage them to go to bed without any clothes but tell them they are not to have any contact with their spouse's genitals or erogenous zones. They are encouraged to gently touch or caress their partner's arms, legs, face, and so on but must agree to postpone intercourse. As a result, all pressure is off, and they learn to focus on the variety of sensations experienced in the moment while mindfully attending to signals of enjoyment, such as "Mmm, that's nice." By the third or fourth night, some limited genital contact is allowed but still no intercourse. Throughout this process, they are becoming more responsive yet without expectations or judgments.

This mindfulness solution worked beautifully for Mike and Megan. By engaging in sensate focus, they learned to seek the other's pleasure, stay in the moment, and soften expectations. They had not had sex in months when they entered marital therapy. She was hurt and angry, and he was checked out and lost his libido. By taking off all pressure to achieve orgasm and learning to listen and discover the pleasure of simple touch, they were able to relax, trust, and enjoy sexual intimacy again. Even though I essentially forbade them to have intercourse for a week, after a few days of sensate focus, they could not resist engaging in coitus. As suggested earlier, it is often not easy to let go of the past. Guilt, regret, or resentment regarding infidelity can easily derail intimacy. Mindfulness can help us make peace with our past and engage in compassion even during lovemaking. To summarize, creating a vibrant and satisfying sex life with our spouse is primarily a function of our ability to be mindful.

Mindfulness Exercise #7

Eye Gaze Meditation

I invite you to try a mindfulness exercise together as a married couple called the "Eye Gaze Meditation." Begin by standing about eighteen to twenty-four inches apart, facing one another, arms resting at your sides. This can feel a bit unusual at first, as the eyes are considered the "windows to the soul." Don't be surprised if you feel a little vulnerable or get a case of the giggles.

Gently close your eyes for a few minutes to simply focus on your breathing. You may sense your spouse's presence, or you may not—either way is okay. After you have developed a bit of concentration, open your eyes and focus on the belly of your spouse. Simply observe his or her breathing as you also notice your own breath in the background. After a few minutes of watching your spouse breathing, bring your gaze up to look into the eyes of the other. Again, if this feels too uncomfortable, it is fine to return to watching the abdomen expand and recede with each breath for a short while. Then return to the eye gaze.

Take a few minutes to simply notice the size, shape, and color of your spouse's eyes without judgment. Rather, pause to appreciate the unique flecks of color that are part of the iris and the size of the pupil. If you or your spouse feels the need to blink, that is perfectly fine. Notice the eyelashes and how the light in the room may reflect off the surface of the eyes.

As you gaze into the eyes of your wife or husband, consider that these eyes once gazed into the eyes of his or her parents or caregivers as an infant. As you softly look into his or her eyes, consider how he or she learned to crawl and later to pull him- or herself up to a standing position and perhaps walked for the first time. Ponder how your spouse began to learn basic words and how to wave hello or goodbye. At one point, his or her greatest achievement was discovering how to tie his or her own shoes.

Imagine your spouse going to school for the first time full of curiosity, caution, and wonder. Envision him or her engaging in a favorite activity as a young boy or girl, yearning to be a part of something and delighting in discovering interests and abilities. Imagine also the first time he or she experienced loss, fear, and disappointment. Perhaps a pet died in grade school or he or she got his or her heart broken as a teenager. These same eyes cried soft tears at the time as he or she experienced those painful emotions.

Now imagine how your spouse will look as he or she advances in age, perhaps experiencing a slowing down or a physical infirmity. One day, your spouse will pass away, and those eyes will close for the last time as he or she transitions to be with the Heavenly Father. Now return to noticing the quality, shape, and color of your spouse's eyes for a short while. Slowly return your gaze to observe the movement of his or her belly as he or she breathes with you. After a couple of minutes, gently close your eyes and focus once again on the rhythmical quality of your own breath.

> But from the beginning of creation, "God made them male and female. For this reason a man shall leave his father and mother [and be joined to his wife], and the two shall become one flesh." So they are no longer two but one flesh. Therefore what God has joined together, no human being must separate.
> —Mark 10:6–9 (NABRE)

CHAPTER 8

Communicating Mindfully

Over the years of practicing mindfulness meditation as a Christian, I have not been seeking to achieve some special state. I am not seeking insight, enlightenment, or even relaxation. Expecting meditation to relax me would represent a judgment, and I am momentarily letting go of judgment. Rather, I find that mindfulness meditation keeps me grounded. It allows me to experience things without reacting to them. It also enables me to be more fully aware since we are liable to miss a lot when we are stuck in our heads with our own negative assumptions and perceptions or merely reacting to nonverbals in our interactions like a "Hmmph!" or a rolling of the eyes.

Mindfulness meditation helps me to live a life worthy of my calling. This idea comes from a scripture in Ephesians. "I, then, a prisoner for the Lord urge you to live in a manner worthy of the call you have received with all humility and gentleness, with patience, bearing with one another through love, striving to preserve the unity of the spirit through the bond of peace" (Ephesians 4:1–3 NABRE). To live a life worthy of your calling is the idea that if I were a garbage man, for instance, then I would be the best garbage man I could be! It does not mean that I will always be in that job or role, but it's not going to change in the next eight hours. So why not give it my full attention? Why not embrace the full experience? Even if all I am doing is emptying garbage cans into a truck all day. It may not be where I would choose to be, but it is where God has me today, so why not give it my all? As St. Theresa of Calcutta was known to say, "Not all of us can do great things. But we can do small things with great love." The calling or vocation where the effort to love in small ways is most frequently required is in marriage. At the heart of a loving, lasting marital relationship is solid communication.

A Pathway to Greater Closeness as a Couple

Effective communication is pivotal in forming and maintaining a strong marriage. Every couple I have ever seen in marital therapy has complained of problems communicating with each other. For that matter, most couples not in therapy share the same concerns. "We can't communicate without fighting." "She does not understand me when I try to talk to her." "It's like we are speaking different languages." "No matter how much I talk to him, he just doesn't get me!" Clearly, communication difficulties are ubiquitous.

Each couple I saw early in my career suggested poor communication was at the root of their problems. So, like a good cognitive-behavioral therapist, I would brilliantly recommend we begin treatment by focusing on communication skills training. I would conduct several sessions of excellent communication training, and, ironically, I would end up with two individuals who were exquisitely articulate at expressing how incredibly unhappy they were with each other. It didn't get them to where they wanted to be. What they truly desire is love, respect, closeness, understanding, appreciation, kindness, gentleness, and security. As it turns out, excellent communication skills will fail us without well-developed abilities in emotional self-regulation. This is our ability to tolerate and express intense feelings, such as anger, sadness, jealousy, and fear, in healthy ways.

Emotional self-regulation may include patience, assertiveness, delay of gratification, distress tolerance, optimism, empathy, stress management, and compassion for self and others. A daily practice of mindfulness can help cultivate all of these resources. It enables me to have the courage to share my feelings one moment and yet the ability to respectfully bite my tongue the next. For example, when my wife criticizes my driving, it often feels like an attack. If I react with anger, it escalates the conflict. If I pause before reacting negatively and realize her motivation for commenting on my driving is to keep me safe, I am able to self-regulate my anger and frustration and not get so defensive. Again, I encourage the reader to consider the words of the Nazi concentration camp survivor Victor Frankl: "Between stimulus and response there is a space. In that space is our power to choose our response. In our response lies our growth and our freedom."

Giving and Receiving Feedback

The book of Proverbs suggests that the wise man welcomes admonishment, but the fool rejects correction. Most of us don't relish negative feedback, especially from family members. However, if I purposefully seek feedback from my spouse, I will become a better husband and father.

Mindful awareness in marriage involves checking in with your spouse. Because of past conflicts and hurts, couples may begin to avoid communication around important issues because they assume it will devolve into defensiveness, criticism, or arguing. Frequent check-ins have three significant advantages. One advantage is I am seeking feedback versus getting unsolicited feedback, which I typically perceive as criticism even if it may be beneficial. Secondly, your partner feels like his or her ideas and opinions are valued and respected. Lastly, mounting problems are avoided because issues are addressed in a timely manner rather than avoided. I remember one couple I treated years ago who did not benefit from my encouragement to take the initiative and check in with each other.

Eddy and Erica were a nice couple in their early thirties. They were both successful in their respective jobs and owned a beautiful home. However, Erica was talkative, and Eddy was quiet. This is not unusual given that, on average, women speak more words per day than men (Pennbaker, 2007). The issue was Eddy refused to talk about problems. Often, he would just shrug his shoulders and remain silent. I offered to meet individually to help Eddy find his voice, but he refused, leaving Erica in the dark. He cared about Erica but continued to do his own thing and would not communicate about their issues. Erica had a health condition she was managing well but needed Eddy's support. In addition, she wanted to spend more time together. After numerous attempts to engage him in dialogue to no avail, Erica decided to leave Eddy. Sadly, their divorce could have been prevented had Eddy been willing to learn how to give and receive feedback. According to Dr. John Gottman, this "openness to influence" is instrumental in developing a satisfying and successful marriage.

There are numerous ways to check in with your spouse. One simple way is to ask your partner how he or she would rate the quality of your closeness or connection from one to ten—one indicating a very poor feeling of connection and ten suggesting fantastic closeness. Don't worry whether your spouse says two or eight. Rather, take a nonjudgmental, proactive approach and ask, "What's one thing I could do today that would take it up one notch from a two to a three", for example. You are not required to do this one thing so you need not get defensive. You are merely gathering information. Your goal is to listen and reflect what was said to ensure you understand the request accurately. Now, if my wife were to say, "Be nicer!" I may need to seek clarification. For instance, I may ask her to paint me a picture by providing some behavioral examples. In other words, "If I were being nicer, what would you see?" I would, again, repeat what I heard she wanted from me without complaining, explaining, or justifying my prior behavior or attitude. Then you would have your partner ask you the one to ten rating question. Remember, the goal of this exercise is not to deliberate the reasonability of the feedback received. Rather, it is to listen and learn mindfully without reacting negatively. Oftentimes, the request was so simple, I wished I had asked the question sooner. If I had only known that doing one or two things would make my spouse feel happier about us and closer to me, I would have done it long ago. Unfortunately, I far too often didn't ask the right question, or I assumed I knew the answer.

I learned this lesson the hard way. I recall one evening years ago when our children were young. My wife was upstairs giving baths and tending to the children. I knew she had had a very busy day, and I wanted to do something nice for her, so I thought, *I know. I'll wash the dishes without being asked!* Ten minutes later, as I was washing the dishes, my wife yelled down the stairs, "Ted! Where are you?"

I proudly responded, "I'm in the kitchen, honey. I'm doing the dishes!"

To which, she responded with an aggravated tone, "Great! I'm caring for the kids all day long, and you come home and all you want is time to yourself!"

I was stunned, confused, and perturbed because my intentions were good. I wanted to be helpful. What did I do wrong? I didn't check in. I failed to communicate effectively. Had I first gone upstairs and simply asked, "How can I help you?" she might have said, "Oh my gosh, if you could bathe the kids, I could get the dishes done," or "I've been stuck in the house all day; let's leave the dishes and go for a walk as a family." For this to happen, I have to open my mouth and elicit information about her needs or feelings. This took me several years to learn because, like so many spouses, I based my decisions on my assumptions or my own needs. Alternatively, we might expect our husband or wife to read our minds and anticipate our needs. In both cases, communication breaks down, and hurt and frustration emerge.

Other ways exist to check in with your spouse. I recommend that you ask your partner this week, "Do you feel loved, honored, and cherished?" And if he or she says, "No," or "I'm not sure," ask, "What can I do to change that?" Again, if you have been meditating daily, you will not rush to judgment or a sense of failure. You will feel much better equipped to listen attentively and restate what you heard to confirm you understood his or her request.

One of my mentors in my career taught me that requests are always received better than complaints. It doesn't guarantee that your request will be granted, but it promotes constructive dialogue about how to get the desired result or behavior. In marriage, there are generally two ways to seek more affection. The first is to complain, "You never touch me anymore!" The other approach is a request. "I miss those times when we'd snuggle on the porch and watch the sunset together. Could we do that again this week?" The first fosters guilt and ill feelings. The second invites possibility and positive images of behavioral change.

My wife, Kathleen, has a beautiful way that she checks in with me. Once or twice a week, often at the end of a busy day, she'll ask, "So how's my best friend?" This is her way of saying "I'm listening." I can say as much or as little as I want, and she will receive it mindfully with gentleness and compassion.

Men's brains seem to be wired for emotional detachment. This is a blessing and a curse. If a couple of men witnessed a car accident and saw smoke and flames coming out of the engine, they would likely shove their feelings aside and pull the people out of the vehicle. A few minutes later, they might experience some fear thinking, *That car could have blown up!* But, initially, they compartmentalize the feelings as secondary to action. This is a cool thing in that instance. However, this same emotional detachment can just kill our marriages because our wives want to know what we are feeling. Oftentimes, when my wife asks how I'm feeling, I honestly don't know. I have to actually stop and examine my heart, and even then, it may not be crystal clear. In contrast, my wife is very perceptive. She seems to always know how she and others are feeling. This is a beautiful thing. The downside is women tend to be more emotionally reactive than men. Once again, a daily practice of mindfulness meditation can help men to be more present and emotionally aware, whereas it can facilitate healthy emotional detachment for women so as to not take things quite so personally. The result is greater openness to feedback and appreciation for each other's gifts.

Marital expert Gary Smalley encourages men to tap into their wife's built-in marriage manual. Whereas men tend to be achievement-oriented, women are naturally relationship-oriented. What may seem like criticisms are often intended to foster stronger families. By checking in a couple of times each week, we typically are encouraged to devote more time and energy to our relationships with our wives and our children. Mindfulness cultivates this kind openness, awareness, and receptivity.

Communication and Connectedness

Nonverbal communication is essential for attunement with your spouse. Nonverbals include posture, facial expressions, and hand gestures, as well as vocal qualities like tone and volume. When someone sneers, throws his or her hands up in disgust, and turns his or her body away, that person's spouse doesn't feel safe or connected. I was recently working with a couple, and when the husband was explaining his efforts, his wife rolled her eyes. He saw this and exploded with "I'm done!" This immediately elicited abandonment fears within her, and the chasm between them widened. We immediately began intensive training in mindfulness, and the marriage was saved. You see, when we face our husband or wife with an open posture and a soft or kind look on our face along with vocal utterances that connote the presence, like "Mmm" or "Uh-huh," it opens the door to attunement. Attunement is the felt sense that your partner is fully present, engaged, and emotionally available. This is at the heart of mindfulness. When parents gaze into the eyes of their infant and respond to their coos with smiles and expressive words as if they were having a conversation, neural networks light up in the baby's brain that foster attachment and healthy cognitive and emotional development. When a husband provides this same kind of mindful attunement, his wife experiences a sense of intimacy and emotional safety. Once they have achieved this, the couple is prepared to join together spiritually.

Mindfulness Exercise #8

Communicating Mindfully

Each spouse should jot down his or her individual responses to each of the following prompts and then sit together to share them afterward:

A. Three things I hope for our love relationship are

1. _____

2. _____

3. _____

B. Two things that I could do this week to promote a better relationship are

1. _____

2. _____

C. One thing I wish you better understood about me is

1. _____

Suggestions

Notice your spouse's responses to each question without debating, evaluating, or defending. Listen mindfully. You need not agree or disagree with his or her opinions or ideas. Attempt to listen with some curiosity and desire to simply understand. Attempts to seek clarification are welcome. Don't feel like you must do any of these things. Rather the goal is primarily to listen and grasp something that is important to your partner.

Be kind to one another, tender-hearted, forgiving each other, just as God in Christ also has forgiven you.

—Ephesians 4:32 (New American Standard Bible)

CHAPTER 9

Spirituality and Marriage

> Always be humble and gentle. Be patient
> with each other, making allowances for each
> other's faults because of your love.
> —Ephesians 4:2 (CLB)

Marriage is a calling to something bigger than yourself. It is not just a piece of paper filed down at the courthouse that can give us some tax advantages. Rather, it is a vocation ultimately designed to give God greater glory. Many young people view relationships in Hollywood terms as a means to an end—that is, fun, excitement, sex, companionship. Others see marriage as a way to fill a void and combat loneliness and isolation. It can be all those things, but it is so much more. Marriage is a living sacrament, a tangible sign of God's grace given to us to help live out our vocation.

American society doesn't seem to be supportive of marriage. Despite empirical evidence that marriage is correlated with better health, increased wealth, academic success for children, and diminished risk of crime and domestic violence, we see many discouraging signs. Popular media rarely portrays healthy loving couples. Most TV spouses are masters of sarcastic put-downs and make a mockery of marriage. Technology continues to promote greater isolation as each spouse gets absorbed in hours of wasted time on social media. I recently saw a married couple at a restaurant, and both were staring at their phones throughout the meal. It saddened me to witness the wasted opportunity to connect as a couple. My wife and I used to watch a show called *ER* until an episode in which a reporter revealed to the rest of the department that Dr. Greene was a virgin when he got married, and they spent the rest of the episode making fun of him. It was the last time we ever watched that show.

These are precisely the reasons why couples need to pray together daily. Romans 12:2 (NABRE) reads, "Do not conform yourselves to this age but be transformed by a renewal of your mind." We are called to be different from the world. What we are positively called to be can be discerned through prayer. It can feel a little awkward at first if you are not accustomed to praying together. I challenge every husband reading this to take the lead and invite your wife to pray with you for a few minutes today! Matthew 18:20 (NASB) asserts, "For where two or three have gathered together in My name, I am there in their midst." What an incredible opportunity to invite Christ into your home, into your marriage, into your hearts! I am surprised to discover how many of the Christian couples I meet in marital therapy have never prayed together. Some fear their spouse will refuse, and some feel it is hypocritical, while others say they have no idea how to get started. I find that a simple, straightforward request works best, like "Honey, would you be willing to pause to pray for a few minutes before we start our day?" If she says no, that's okay; pause and pray yourself.

Praying together need not be anything formal or fancy. Often we will offer up a few intentions for family and friends who are going through a difficult time. We might pray for our church, community, workplace, or nation. It is particularly meaningful to pray for God's healing, blessing, and protection of our marriage. We might end by saying an "Our Father" together. Other couples may prefer more structured prayer. As Catholics, we will often say a rosary together. The rosary is a meditation on the life of Christ. I frequently tell my clients that meditation can deepen one's prayer life because there is a significant difference between saying a rosary and praying a rosary. With the former, I may just be rattling off familiar prayers while my mind is elsewhere. With the latter, I am meditating on an event in the life of Jesus for those ten "Hail Marys." I have always agreed with the old adage that a family that prays together stays together!

Praying alone with your spouse is a shared activity that fosters intimacy. Typically, we will be sitting beside one another. Often, we will hold hands as we present our needs, hopes, and fears to a God who listens and loves us. We may learn what is weighing on the heart of our spouse by the content of his or her prayers. As you join together in sincere prayer, your wife or husband feels your support and concern. We have a family tradition of making the sign of the cross on the forehead of each of our children when they go to bed or leave on a trip. Sometimes, my wife or I will bless each other in this way before we go to sleep, and we find it to be tender and comforting.

Aside from asking God's forgiveness for times we have fallen short of His order and plans for our lives, I feel the most significant aspect of prayer is expressing gratitude. In a sense, every day is Thanksgiving—a time to be mindful of all the blessings God has bestowed on us individually and collectively. When a married couple is struggling with hurt, anger, or emotional disconnect, giving thanks may be the furthest thing from our minds. Yet mindfulness allows us to become aware of so much that we are missing because of our preoccupation with a snide remark, hurtful event from the past, or anxiety about the future. My wife, Kathleen, taught me the value of counting my blessings. When doing therapy with an individual or a couple, I will periodically ask them to make a gratitude list. They may find this task difficult at first because they are upset about past offenses or worried about feeling miserable years from now if their spouse does not change. The list may start out slowly. "I am grateful my car started up this morning and that I have enough to eat and a roof over my head." But if I encourage them to continue, they realize other blessings like vision and hearing, friends, employment, or living in a free country. Within several minutes, they have filled a page with things for which they are grateful. As a result, their mood, attitude, and entire perspective have noticeably improved.

In the marital health group I conduct with my couples, I have them do a "faith walk" in which half of the participants are blindfolded. Their "mystery guide" remains silent while they take them on a ten-minute walk through the building. Then they switch blindfolds, and the other half goes on a faith walk not knowing who their guide is. This leads to a rich discussion about trust, confusion, faith, and disorientation. Some report it to be a very uncomfortable experience to put their trust in someone they can neither see nor hear and may hardly know. Typically, after several minutes, the blindfolded one lets go and realizes the guide has no intention to harm him or her. In addition, some attunement develops as they discern nonverbal ways to communicate and guide them through doorways, up stairs, and onto elevators on their faith walk. This can become a metaphor for trust in their marriage as well as trust in God. Remember that we "walk by faith, not by sight" (2 Cor 5:7 NASB).

The Spiritual Exercises of Saint Ignatius were designed as a thirty-day meditation program designed to deepen one's relationship with God and incorporate these habits into one's daily life. One entire day is spent contemplating the question, "How clearly do I see God in all things?" Another day is spent meditating on "How clearly do I see God's love in all things?" A daily mindfulness meditation practice prepares the heart and mind to embrace these challenging questions. In fact, these awarenesses are a natural outcome or extension of a mindfulness practice. In other words, we are able to see the sacred in the ordinary. Sometimes, I will be engaged in the breath meditation outlined in chapter 1, and I will find myself spontaneously thanking God for each breath. The truth be told, I can go for days without even thinking once about my breath, but if I didn't breathe for three or four minutes, I wouldn't even be here! When you can begin to see God's love and creativity in the uniqueness of your spouse, you are well on your way to a stronger, more intimate marital relationship.

Incorporating God's Wisdom into Your Marital Relationship

God designed humans for relationships. The more we learn about the brain and cognitive development, the more we realize how God built us to be in intimate connection to Him and one another. This has implications for the company you keep, as some relationships are edifying and some are diminishing or discouraging. I routinely encourage my marital therapy couples to "hang with the happy."

My wife and I went to a cookout at the home of some old friends. Although it was nice to reminisce with them a bit, the couple bickered, criticized, and made cutting remarks about each other all evening. The sarcastic put-downs were so persistent, it felt like a vexation to my spirit. Perhaps they were trying to be funny, but we decided to distance ourselves from them for a few years and associate with couples who demonstrated love and respect toward their spouse. We found this not only made for a more pleasant evening, but it represented positive role-modeling and an unspoken challenge to do the same.

Proverbs 27:17 (NASB) reads, "Iron sharpens iron, so one man sharpens another." In other words, husbands need other good men in their lives to encourage them to love their wives, employing God's definition of love outlined in 1 Corinthians 13: "Love is gentle, love is kind ..." Many of us chose this reading as a part of our wedding ceremony. Living it out is not easy when relationship problems arise. Remaining mindful of our vows is vital. When we are discouraged, self-absorbed, upset, or feel disconnected from our wives, a true friend will provide healthy admonishment. Modernist thinking would suggest "whatever feels good or feels right to you is okay." A true friend challenges you to be the best person you can be. This could mean avoiding compromising situations with other women; avoiding drunkenness, which impairs a man's judgment; or avoiding pornography, which is demeaning to women and an affront to your wife. On the positive side, a true friend will encourage his friend to set aside quality time for his wife, urge church involvement, or support meaningful communication and openness to feedback.

I mentioned at the outset of this chapter that marriage is a calling to something bigger than ourselves. Engaging in an activity that benefits others binds a couple together and creates shared meaning. A simple suggestion would be volunteering together. My wife and I will periodically give a talk to young couples preparing for marriage. We might volunteer to work a refreshment stand or stock shelves at the Parish Food Pantry together. Recently, we led a group of fifteen teens preparing for their Confirmation so they can learn how to live a life in the Spirit of God as emerging members of our faith community. This is the equivalent of working on God's farm side by side as a couple. To be His hands and feet in the world and bring people closer to Him is also known as "the Great Commission."

Mindfulness Exercise #9

Scripture Meditation

Begin by finding a quiet place to sit and pick a word, phrase, or verse from Holy Scripture as we are all called to meditate upon God's word. A nice suggestion is Psalm 46:11 (NABRE): "Be still and know that I am God!" Once you have gotten centered, begin quietly synchronizing the two parts of this verse with each inhalation and exhalation. Thus, as you breathe in, think, *Be still*, and as you breathe out, think, *and know that I am God*. Do not attempt to interpret or analyze the content of the verse, but just allow the simple words to resonate within your heart. You are not trying to feel a certain way or understand something deep and mysterious. Rather by sitting with the words with an open, nonjudging mind-set, you allow God to reveal Himself to you in His own unique way. Should you get distracted, just note this and return to the breath and these simple words from Psalms. See if you can sustain this soft focus for about fifteen minutes each morning this week. Next week, pick a new verse, such as "I can do all things through Christ who gives me strength" (Philippians 4:13).

Let the words of my mouth and the meditations of my heart be pleasing to you, Lord, my rock and my redeemer.

—Psalm 19:14 (Common English Bible)

Chapter 10

The Great Commission

My friend Dan once said at a Parish Council meeting at church, "Of all the things we discuss and do, our number-one objective is to get more people into heaven." I thought it was a simple, direct comment that cut right to the heart of the matter. I would suggest it all starts at home. One of my greatest overarching concerns should be getting my wife into heaven. I figure just the fact that she has put up with me all these years should get her straight into heaven no questions asked! Seriously, the Great Commission refers to Jesus's last words to His apostles before His ascension into heaven. "All authority in heaven and earth has been given to me. Therefore go and make disciples of all the nations, baptizing them in the name of the Father and of the Son and of the Holy Spirit, and teaching them to obey everything I have commanded you. And surely I am with you always, to the very end of the age" (Matthew 28:18–20 NIV). We want to help others encounter Christ in a personal way.

I have always believed that a healthy marriage is the foundation for a healthy family and a healthy family is the basis for a healthy society. This idea is corroborated by the sociological data available in the United States. If one were to solely examine the effects of a boy or girl growing up without a father in the home, the significance of intact families becomes evident. Research by the National Center for Fathering demonstrates that "children from fatherless homes are more likely to be poor, become involved in drug and alcohol abuse, drop out of school and suffer from health and emotional problems. Boys are more likely to become involved in crime and girls are more likely to become pregnant as teens." (www.fathers.com) There are multiple ways to explain this data, but clearly when Dad loves Mom and Mom loves Dad, it creates a deep sense of security within their children that promotes health and welfare in numerous ways over the course of their lives. The family becomes a safe harbor from which they can venture forth to fulfill God's purposes in their lives.

Cultivating mindfulness can be an enormous blessing in developing a resilient, growing, loving marriage. My wife and I had a fight this morning, but as a result of our mindfulness practices, we were able to be mindful of our deep love and refocus on the issue at hand. Our skillfulness in mindfulness meditation enabled us to access inner resources of empathy, owning feelings, and making requests versus just reacting based on fear or mistaken assumptions. Years ago, a fight of this magnitude may have prompted a cold, bitter emotional disconnect for days. Today, we were able to do repair work and reconnect within several minutes. By God's grace, we were able to say, "I'm sorry we fought. I'm sorry I yelled at you. I love you. I don't want to fight with you. We can figure this out." Within seconds, emotional safety began to steadily increase. We were able to embrace and comfort each other. Our kids weren't home this morning, but they have seen us fight and seen us reconcile and stick by one another through thick and thin. This also sends a powerful message about perseverance in love for the next generation. Our efforts to strengthen our marriage through mindfulness edify the future vocation of our children.

Marriage is a microcosm of the world. Struggles between countries and races are not that different from the core of conflicts in marital relationships. As mentioned in chapter 3, coming to understand and appreciate differences can go a long way toward resolving conflicts and restoring trust and effective communication. We can do our part in promoting world peace by restoring peace in our own homes. My wife sometimes holds a mirror up to my face, metaphorically, and I don't always like what I see. My attitude, words, behaviors, and even facial expressions can be ugly, scornful, and rejecting at times. Marriage and parenting can bring out the best and the worst in me. It can expose all my defects: selfishness, avoidance, hostility, defensiveness, criticism, blaming, and so on. Left to my own devices, I can make terrible decisions. This is why I so desperately need a savior in my life. If I am open to growth and realize God is continually molding me, I will avail myself of His pruning and become the husband He wants me to be. As I have said before, success in marriage is not so much about finding the right person as it is about being the right person.

Creating or restoring peace in my home starts with me identifying, acknowledging, and weeding out my defects of character. Prayer and mindfulness meditation can empower me to love my wife as she deserves. This can foster harmony with one another. Even though I may be a baritone and she may be an alto, we can sing God's praises with one voice as suggested in the following passage from Romans.

> Brothers and sisters: Whatever was written previously was written for our instruction, that by endurance and by the encouragement of the scriptures we might have hope. May the God of endurance and encouragement grant you to think in harmony with one another, in keeping with Christ Jesus, that with one accord you may with one voice glorify the God and Father of our Lord Jesus Christ. Welcome one another, then, as Christ welcomed you, for the glory of God. (Romans 15:4–8 NIV)

We Are His Hands and Feet Leading by Example

God provides the "endurance and encouragement" we need to work together in "one accord." Our marriage can become a beacon of light for other married couples. My wife and I recently went on a retreat together. At the end of the retreat, multiple people told us they hope that they can create a marital relationship like ours based on how they observed us treating each other with kindness and respect. We had no idea we were subtly modeling love for others.

I recall as a young child singing the following lyrics to a song at church. "They'll know we are Christians by our love." Similarly, St. Francis of Assisi in sending out his friars to the corners of the earth, purportedly instructed them, "Preach Jesus, and if necessary use words." Both admonitions can be achieved by fulfilling your wedding vows to love your spouse through thick and thin. Most people would agree it is easier to show love to a total stranger than to treat your spouse lovingly when you are not getting along. Imagine what a witness this could be to our children, neighbors, and friends if we could demonstrate agape in our marriage. Agape is the highest form of love or charity. Wikipedia suggests "agape embraces a universal, unconditional love that transcends, that serves regardless of circumstances." (en.wikipedia.org>wiki>Agape)

We knew a woman in our neighborhood named Margaret who had a medical condition that prevented her from sitting up. As a result, she was bedridden for over thirty years. She never complained but spent her days praying for others. Her husband kindly tended to her every need. John 15:3 reads, "Greater love hath no man than this, that a man lay down his life for his friends." This humble, quiet couple modeled agape for me. I hope every person who reads this realizes this powerful opportunity to lead by example and inspire younger married couples to walk the talk.

I have known quite a few men and women who loved their spouse but had trouble showing it or communicating that love through their behavior and attitudes. Mindfulness meditation is well known to foster compassion. It starts with our initial efforts to struggle through developing a daily practice of meditation. Thirty years ago, I would get frustrated with myself when meditating. I'd think, *Gosh, Ted, you can't even stay focused on your breath for ten seconds without getting distracted!* However, over the course of time, my heart softened, and I came to accept my own distractibility. My response changed to *Oh, I must have gotten off track. That happens sometimes*, and I gently take my awareness by the hand and guide it back to the breath or whatever my focal point is. As the years passed, I discovered it became easier and easier to extend this sort of compassion to others even under challenging circumstances.

If you have gone through difficult times as a couple and reconciled, other couples may benefit greatly from your willingness to share your pain and your joy. This is the Holy Spirit at work in your life. I have always been drawn to healthy couples who treat one another with love and respect. On the surface, it may seem like they have no problems, but, undoubtedly, they have endured, grown, and sometimes thrived through the relationship adversity. When an opportunity arises to minister to a couple who is suffering through conflict, betrayal, or boredom, don't preach, but, rather, lead by example. You might say, "I don't know what's right for you, but I can tell you a few things that were healing when our marriage was on the rocks," like mindfulness and praying together. Holy Scripture urges us to be a light in a darkened world. "For you were once darkness, but now you are light in the Lord. Live as children of the light, for light produces every kind of goodness and righteousness and truth. Try to learn what is pleasing to the Lord" (Ephesians 5:8–10 NABRE). In other words, as a result of your awakening to the moment, you can be a beacon of light that points the way for other couples. Through your example and testimony, other couples can learn how to sustain a healthy marriage through the practice of mindfulness in everyday life.

Psalm 118:24 (ESV) reads, "This is the day that the Lord has made: Let us rejoice and be glad *in it*." I added the emphasis to the last two words "*in it*" to highlight an important aspect of Christian mindfulness. Life does not always go easily. Things often do not go as planned. Many of us envisioned years of wedded bliss on our wedding day only to remark years later that marriage is much harder than we thought it would be. Nevertheless, we can learn through mindfulness to embrace each day with openness and compassion, knowing the Lord made this day uniquely for each of us. This is my time with my spouse—to have and to hold, to honor and cherish, to be an example of Christian love, patience, and fidelity. To me, this scripture suggests we can *choose* to rejoice and be glad in this very day regardless of our relationship circumstances. In Philippians 4:4 (NIV), St. Paul urges us to "Rejoice in the Lord always. I will say it again: Rejoice!" Chances are that Paul was chained to a dungeon wall when he wrote this, as he spent much of his ministry in captivity because he refused to stop preaching in the name of Christ Jesus. Joy is not the opposite of sorrow. I have known many who have praised God in all things and rejoiced in the Lord even in the midst of trials, suffering, or painful losses. If we attempt to manage in one day all the regrets from the past and all the anticipated suffering in the future, it can be overwhelming. However, if we remain in *this* day with what God is calling us to do now and place the past and all of our future worries in His loving hands, we can truly seize the day and rejoice in it!

As the book draws to a conclusion, I urge you to maintain a daily practice of mindfulness meditation. I usually encourage a dedicated time each morning to a sitting practice, as it can set the tone for the day. If the morning gets away from you, look for opportunities to incorporate mindfulness into everyday activities, as this is the goal in the long run. The other evening, I was feeling stressed and drained from a hard day at work. Even though it was 9:00 p.m. on a cold, snowy night, I asked my wife if she'd go for a walk with me. She agreed, so we bundled up and went for a hike through the woods by our house. We came to an observation deck overlooking a marsh and stood together in silence for almost fifteen minutes without uttering a word. The silence and the stillness were amazing. The only movement was the softly falling snowflakes.

I suggested picking out a single snowflake and visually following it from high in the sky until it landed on the frozen surface of the pond. Not only was this precious time shared together as a couple, it was a chance to practice meditation. By focusing on one thing, remaining in the moment, without judging, I experienced a deep sense of serenity and centeredness. Beyond that, I gained freedom from all anxiety just as Jesus taught when He instructed us to "consider the sparrows." Lastly, I discovered gratitude to and appreciation of God for the uniqueness of each snowflake. Learning mindfulness is a pathway to being fully present to your spouse. Being fully present is the best gift you can give your spouse. Thank you for your courage and perseverance in interweaving mindfulness into your marriage!

Mindfulness Exercise #10

Dancing Mindfully

I invite the husband to find a quiet moment this evening and pick out one of your wife's favorite slow-dance songs. Turn down the lights in the living room, and ask your wife for a dance. Don't judge whether you believe you are good dancer or not. Simply hold your wife and sway gently to the rhythm of the music. Notice how it feels to hold your love in your arms. Don't get caught up reminiscing ruefully about simpler times in life or worried that something that feels nice won't last. Rather, observe how easily the two of you sway back and forth to the time of the music with gentleness and compassion. On the final day of the Marital Health Treatment Program I conduct at work, I give each couple a CD of twenty great slow-dance songs and instruct the husband to invite his wife for a dance once a week for the rest of their lives. I have found they all love to slow dance but often have not danced together in years. Making these positive connections a routine part of our lives helps maintain a lasting sense of closeness and resilience that helps sustain us through all of the ups and downs of life.

Have I not commanded you? Be strong and courageous.
Do not be afraid; do not be discouraged, for the
Lord your God will be with you wherever you go.

—Joshua 1:9 (NIV)